BEAD EMBROIDERY

The Complete Guide

Jane Davis

©2005 Jane Davis
Published by

kp **krause publications**
An Imprint of F+W Publications

700 East State Street • Iola, WI 54990-0001
715-445-2214 • 888-457-2873
www.krausebooks.com

Our toll-free number to place an order or obtain a free catalog is
(800) 258-0929.

Library of Congress Catalog Number: 2005906839

ISBN 13-digit: 978-0-87349-888-3
ISBN 10-digit: 0-87349-888-7

Edited by Maria L. Turner and Sarah Herman
Designed by Emily Adler

Printed in China

Acknowledgments

Thank you Sarah Herman and Maria Turner, my wonderful, talented editors, for all of your work on this book.

Thank you Emily Adler for your wonderful layout that makes these pages beautiful.

Thank you Carole Tripp for your help with bead colors and moral support; it is so good to have you as a friend.

Thank you to the fabulous beadwork artists who have allowed me to present their beautiful work in the Gallery section of this book: Wendy Ellsworth, Margo Field, Carol Perrenoud, Jennifer Gallagher and Corinne Loomer.

Thank you to Corinne Loomer for pointing out that beaded cabochons are related as much to bead embroidery as they are to beadwork.

Thank you to Rich, Andrew, Jonathan and Jeff for putting up with deadline after deadline.

Table of Contents

Introduction

Embroidery is a wonderful, multifaceted means of embellishing and beautifying our surroundings. Throughout the history of humankind, embroidery has enriched and enlightened our lives. From the first stitch worked by a nameless ancestor to decorate a piece of clothing or other personal item, embroidery has been a form of creative expression. Whatever led that first inspired person to add a decorative stitch or two above and beyond the laborious task of creating the garment itself shows a drive and ambition that we all have: to be creative and make things our own.

Embroidery has evolved through the centuries, riding a roller coaster of cultures and taste, and at its best, portraying beauty and intricacy, becoming a work of art, and celebrating the heart and soul of the human spirit through color, texture and skill. With this book, I hope to add to that legacy by exploring embroidery from a bead-related view.

Traditionally, beads have been added to fabric with simple stitches, like the backstitch, running stitch or couching stitch. There are, of course, specific beadwork stitches, such as the peyote and brick stitch, which create beaded items without using fabric. This book explores adding beads to common embroidery stitches for a variety of needlework techniques and beading stitches stemming from fabric. Some of the stitches are old and traditional, while others are fairly new.

In the world of embroidery, each stitch has its own character that dictates to some degree how beads can be used in the stitching technique. For instance, you can be creative with Hardanger, but experimenting too much will lead to something that is Hardanger-inspired, but not Hardanger. Other embroidery styles, like freeform embroidery, can be worked either traditionally or experimentally without changing the look of the stitch. This book explores a variety of techniques, from enhancing the traditional to exploring the new and evolving, with the hopes of presenting ideas to inspire you.

In organizing the layout of this book, I have strived for ease in use and as much information as I can get into these pages. The Stitches at a Glance section is a quick reference for any stitch in the book, while the Basics section provides you with the tools, materials and techniques to get started. The Stitches section categorizes the stitches by type, such as counted thread or freeform embroidery. Clear photos show the individual stitches worked up both with and without beads, and sometimes including a variety of options. Finally, the Projects section has 20 projects that show how to incorporate beads into your embroidery work, and the Gallery at the back presents a sampling of more bead embroidery ideas by several bead artists.

My hope is that this book will serve as a handy reference to all those, like me, who enjoy working with beads and thread, and who are always looking for new ways to make beautiful things to enrich our lives and the lives of those around us.

Happy bead embroidering,
Jane Davis

Section 1: Basics

This section holds all the information you need to get started in bead embroidery. From the Stitches at a Glance, an easy stitch guide, to the tools, materials and techniques, it's all here to get you started.

Stitches at a Glance

This quick-reference photo log of all the stitches in the book will come in handy when looking for bead embroidery ideas or trying to find a specific stitch. The photos are organized the same as The Stitches section on page 48 (by stitch type), and show the stitch name and page number.

Needlepoint

1. Tent, page 49

2. Cross, page 50

3. St. George's Cross, page 50

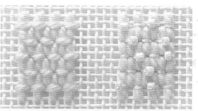

4. Long Upright Cross, page 51

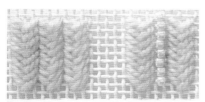

5. Fern, page 51

6. Van Dyke, page 52

7. Slanting Gobelin, page 52

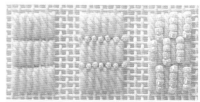

8. Upright Gobelin, page 53

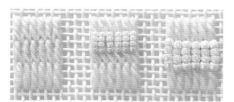

9. Split Upright Gobelin, page 53

10. Encroaching Upright Gobelin, page 54

11. Interlocking Upright Gobelin, page 54

12. Cashmere, page 55

13. Framed Cashmere, page 55

14. Cashmere Checker, page 56

15. Reversed Cashmere, page 56

16. Diagonal Cashmere, page 57

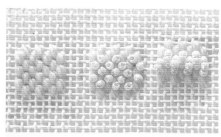

17. Brick, page 57

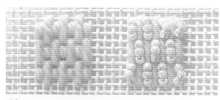

18. Parisian, page 58

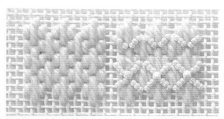

19. Hungarian, page 58

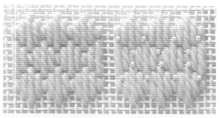

20. Pavilion, page 59

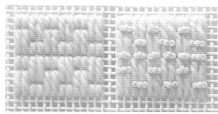

21. Beaty, page 59

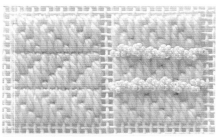

22. Wild Goose Chase, page 60

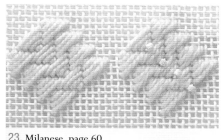

23. Milanese, page 60

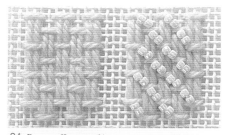

24. Roman II, page 61

25. Pavilion Steps, page 61

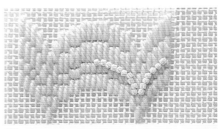

26. Florentine, page 62

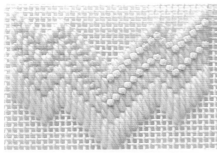

27. Florentine Variation, page 62

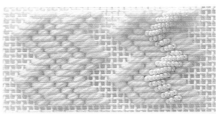

28. Medieval Mosaic, page 63

29. Byzantine, page 63

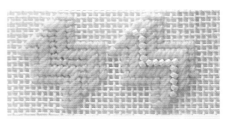

30. Jacquard, page 64

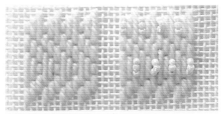

31. Oriental, page 64

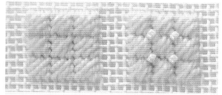

32. Scotch, page 65

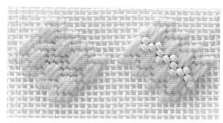

33. Moorish, page 65

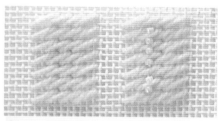

34. Oblique Slav, page 66

35. Kalem, page 66

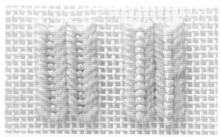

36. Stem, page 67

37. Leaf, page 67

Counted Thread

38. Backstitch, page 68

39. Half Cross, page 69

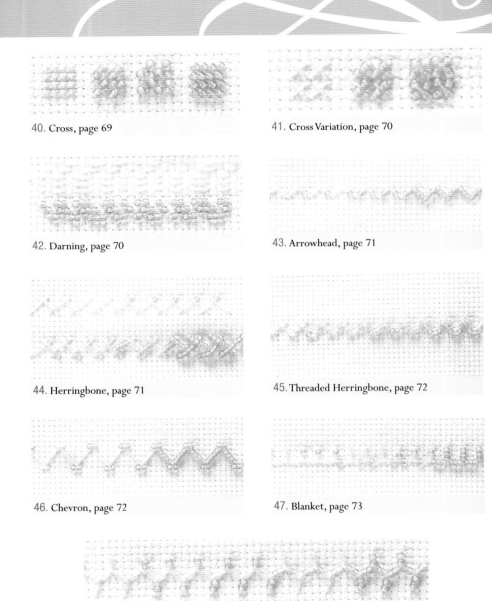

40. Cross, page 69

41. Cross Variation, page 70

42. Darning, page 70

43. Arrowhead, page 71

44. Herringbone, page 71

45. Threaded Herringbone, page 72

46. Chevron, page 72

47. Blanket, page 73

48. Cretan, page 73

Pulled Thread, Drawn Work and Insertion Stitches

Pulled Thread

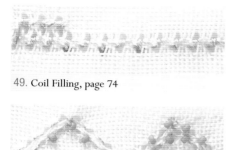

49. Coil Filling, page 74

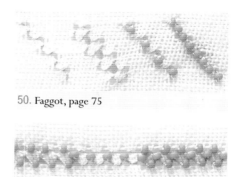

50. Faggot, page 75

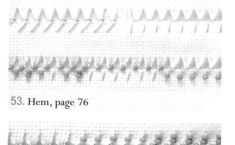

51. Diagonal Chained Border, page 75

52. Four-Sided, page 76

Drawn Work

53. Hem, page 76

54. Ladder Hem, page 77

55. Zigzag Hem, page 77

56. Italian Hem Variation, page 78

57. Interlaced Hem, page 78

Insertion Stitches

58. Cross, page 79

59. Zigzag, page 79

60. Threaded Zigzag, page 80

61. Half Cretan Insertion, page 80

62. Open Cretan Insertion, page 81

63. Knotted Insertion, page 81

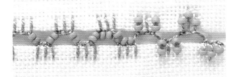

64. Grouped Blanket Insertion, page 82

Hardanger

65. Kloster Blocks, page 83

66. Kloster Square, page 84

67. Small Star Motif, page 84

68. Large Star Motif, page 85

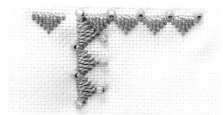

69. Diamond Motif, page 85

70. Triangle Border, page 86

71. Tulip Variation, page 86

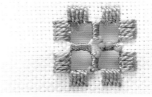

72. Wrapped Bar, page 87

73. Woven Bar, page 87

74. Woven Bar with Picot, page 88

75. Dove's Eye Filling, page 88

Freeform Embroidery

76. Running, page 89

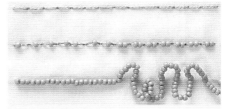

77. Backstitch, page 90

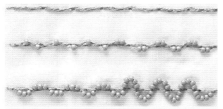

78. Threaded Backstitch, page 90

79. Double Threaded Backstitch, page 91

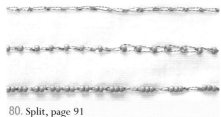

80. Split, page 91

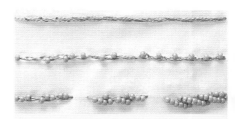

81. Stem, page 92

82. Straight, page 92

83. Seed, page 93

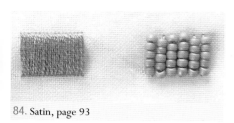

84. Satin, page 93

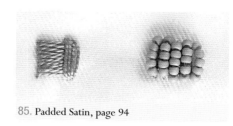

85. Padded Satin, page 94

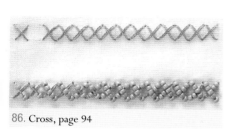

86. Cross, page 94

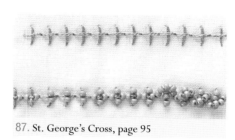

87. St. George's Cross, page 95

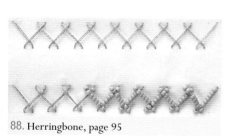

88. Herringbone, page 95

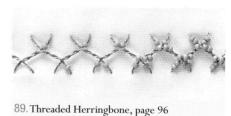

89. Threaded Herringbone, page 96

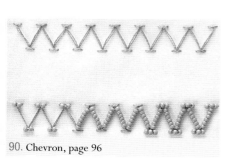

90. Chevron, page 96

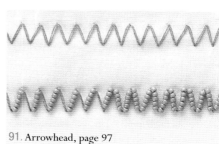

91. Arrowhead, page 97

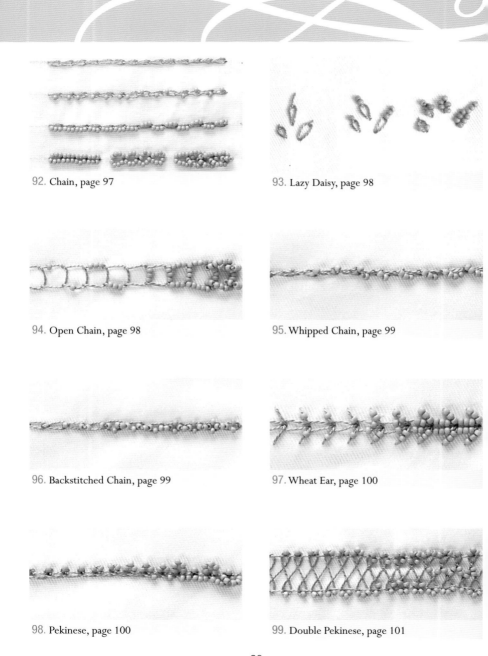

92. Chain, page 97

93. Lazy Daisy, page 98

94. Open Chain, page 98

95. Whipped Chain, page 99

96. Backstitched Chain, page 99

97. Wheat Ear, page 100

98. Pekinese, page 100

99. Double Pekinese, page 101

100. Sheaf, page 101

101. Lock, page 102

102. Fishbone, page 102

103. Fern, page 103

104. Leaf, page 103

105. Romanian, page 104

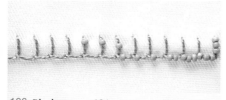

106. Blanket, page 104

107. Buttonhole, page 105

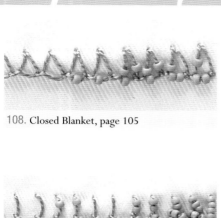

108. Closed Blanket, page 105

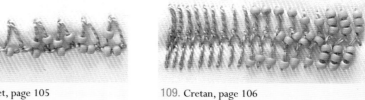

109. Cretan, page 106

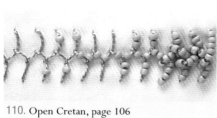

110. Open Cretan, page 106

111. Fly, page 107

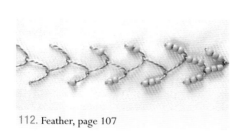

112. Feather, page 107

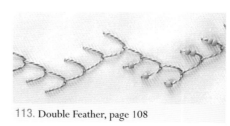

113. Double Feather, page 108

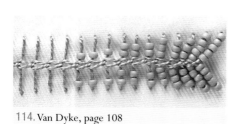

114. Van Dyke, page 108

115. French Knot, page 109

116. Turkey Work, page 109

117. Cloud Filling, page 110

118. Coral, page 110

119. Couching, page 111

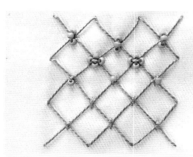

120. Couched Filling, page 111

Crazy Quilt Stitches

121. Overlapping Blanket, page 112

122. Long-and-Short Blanket, page 113

123. Slanted Blanket, page 113

124. Picot Blanket, page 114

125. Two-Sided Blanket, page 114

126. Grouped Blanket, page 115

127. Feathered Blanket, page 115

128. Embellished Feathered Blanket, page 116

129. Wave Blanket, page 116

130. Fanned Buttonhole, page 117

131. Lazy Daisy Buttonhole, page 117

132. Overlapping Chevron, page 118

133. Slanted Cretan, page 118

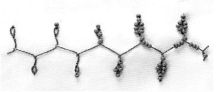

134. Lazy Daisy Cretan, page 119

135. Lazy Daisy Leaf, page 119

136. Lazy Daisy Flower, page 120

137. Fan, page 120

138. Feather, page 121

139. Feather Vine, page 121

140. Flowered Feather, page 122

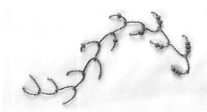

141. Meandering Feather, page 122

142. Herringbone, page 123

143. Herringbone and Blossoms, page 123

144. Herringbone and Leaves, page 124

145. Overlapping Herringbone, page 124

146. Twisted Herringbone, page 125

147. Rosette, page 125

148. Rosette Vine, page 126

149. Rosettes in a Row, page 126

Smocking Stitches

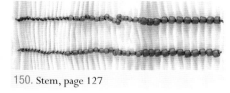

150. Stem, page 127

151. Cable, page 128

152. Double Cable, page 128

153. Wave, page 129

154. Trellis, page 129

155. Feather, page 130

156. Van Dyke, page 130

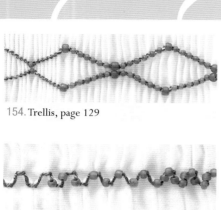

157. Diamond, page 131

158. Crossed Diamond, page 131

159. Surface Honeycomb, page 132

160. Honeycomb, page 132

161. Stacked Triangle, page 133

162. Stacked Diamond, page 133

163. Stacked Heart, page 133

Ribbonwork

164. Running, page 134

165. Ribbon Straight, page 135

166. Couching, page 136

167. French Knot, page 136

168. French Knot Variation, page 137

169. Cross, page 137

170. Fly, page 138

171. Lazy Daisy, page 138

172. Lazy Daisy Variation, page 139

173. Plume, page 139

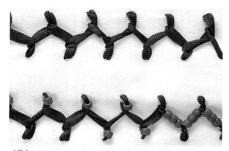

174. Cretan, page 140

175. Sheaf, page 140

Beadwork Stitches

176. Peyote, page 141

177. Brick, page 142

178. Herringbone, page 142

179. Right-Angle Weave, page 143

180. Netting, page 143

Elements for Flowers

181. Stamens, page 144

182. Hanging and Stationary Flowers, page 145

183. Flower Buds, page 146

184. Building Flowers from Several Beads, page 146

185. Attaching Leaves, page 147

186. Seed Bead Leaves, page 148

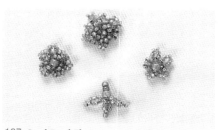

187. Seed Bead Flowers, page 149

Fringes and Edgings

188. One-Row Brick, page 150

189. Picot Brick, page 151

190. Peyote Edge, page 152

191. Herringbone, page 153

192. Classic Edge, page 154

193. Classic Spaced Variation, page 154

194. Shallow Loops, page 155

195. Two-Row Tapered Horizontal Netting, page 155

196. Tapered Three-Row Horizontal Netting, page 156

197. Horizontal Netting with Dangles, page 157

198. Classic Picot, page 158

199. Classic Picot Crowded Variation, page 158

200. Classic Picot Bugle Bead Variation, page 159

201. Overlapping Loops, page 159

202. Overlapping Loops with Dagger Variation, page 160

203. Crowded Overlapping Loops on Curve, page 160

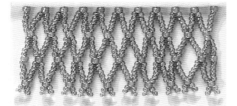

204. Vertical Netting, page 161

205. Vertical Netting with Bugle Beads, page 161

206. Classic Dangle Fringe, page 162

207. Classic Dangle Fringe Variation, page 162

208. Classic Fringe with Swarovski Cube Detail,
page 163

209. Zigzag Fringe Variation, page 163

210. Tapered Fringe Variation,
page 164

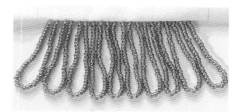

212. Classic Looped Fringe, page 165

211. Dangle Detail, page 164

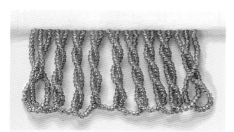

213. Classic Twisted Looped Fringe, page 165

214. Classic Twisted Fringe, page 166

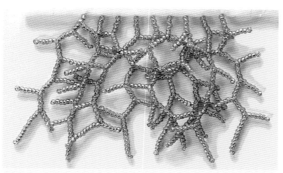

215. Branched Fringe, page 166

Tools and Materials

Incorporating beads into embroidery is a fun and creative process. It also adds to the considerations of tools and materials needed for each project. You will need to choose which types of beads, threads and fabrics to use, and then set up a workspace to handle all those roly-poly bits of glass alongside your threads and fabrics.

Beads

There are many types of beads — some with large holes, some with small holes and some with square holes. When you are planning to embroider with beads, there are several things you need to consider.

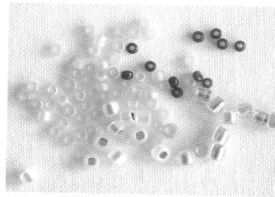

Large-, small- and square-holed beads.

The most commonly used seed beads, and in the middle, size 22 antique seed beads. Clockwise from the top: Size 11 seed beads; size 8 seed beads; size 6 seed beads; size 15 seed beads.

Choosing the Right-Sized Beads for a Project

Readily available beads for beadwork, which are also suitable for bead embroidery, range from size 15 beads, which are about ¹⁄₁₆" (1.5mm) in diameter, to size 6 beads, which are just less than ¼" (5mm) in diameter. Other beads include tiny antique beads that go down to size 24, verging on the size of a grain of salt, and large beads of many different materials including clay, wood, glass, metal, resin or plastic. The stitches shown in this book use mostly size 8 seed beads, about ⅛" (3mm), or size 11 seed beads, about ¹⁄₁₆" (2mm).

Beads are not all uniform, so the size of the outside diameter of the bead doesn't necessarily mean you will be able to get the needle through the hole. Some beads of the same size have smaller holes than others. That is why it is important to make a test swatch with the beads, needles, thread and fabric you intend to use to see if everything works well together. You will often find that even after you've tested your beads, there will be some in your pile that just have smaller holes than the rest and won't get past the eye of the needle. Simply set them aside as you find them and save them for a different project that can accommodate the smaller bead hole.

A variety of beads.

Types of Beads

The majority of beads on the market today are either made in Japan (using machine methods) or the Czech Republic (using traditional bead-making techniques). Two common types of beads work well for embroidery: seed beads and Japanese cylinder beads. Many other types of beads can be added to your stitching for added accents and details.

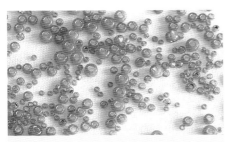

Seed beads.

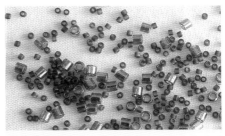

Delica beads.

Seed Beads

Seed beads resemble a doughnut shape and can be irregular or fairly uniform, depending on how they are made. Seed beads made from the Czech Republic or France are generally more rounded, not as uniform in size and have a smaller hole than Japanese-made beads. Seed beads made in Japan are generally a little more cylindrical and more uniform, with a larger hole than the same-sized Czech bead. Any of these seed beads work wonderfully in bead embroidery, but consider the qualities of each when planning your project and choosing your needles and thread.

Cylinder Beads

Japanese cylinder beads, most commonly called Delicas, are machine-made cylinders with large holes compared to the same-diameter seed bead. The Delica brand is made by the Miyuki company, while the Toho or Antique brand beads are made by the Toho company. Cylinder beads are available in two sizes — one similar to a size 11 seed bead and one similar to a size 8 seed bead. Delicas work well for stacked stitches in beadwork, such as peyote or brick stitch, because they fit together neatly like little bricks. They also can be used for all types of embroidery, though the look of the project will be slightly different than the same project worked with rounded seed beads.

Teardrop beads.

Dagger beads.

Faceted beads.

Teardrop Beads

Teardrop beads are shaped like a teardrop, with a side-drilled hole, drilled through the small end of the tapered shape. They are great for dangles, edges and fringes. They also work well as grapes or flowers.

Dagger Beads

Dagger beads are a type of drop bead that is shaped like a sword or dagger with a side-drilled hole, making them classic for fringes and dangles.

Faceted Beads

Faceted beads can be made of crystal (Austrian Swarovski crystals, for example) or cut glass, and add sparkle to any project.

Pressed glass beads.

Triangle beads.

Bugle beads.

Pressed Glass Beads

Pressed glass beads are made in a variety of shapes from abstracts to leaves and flowers. The Toho company makes them as charms for embroidery projects.

Triangle Beads

Triangle beads have a round or triangular hole and are triangular on the outside, looking down the hole. They create an undulating irregular surface that reflects the light.

Bugle Beads

Bugle beads are cylinders that can be either long or short. One bugle bead can be used in place of three or more seed beads in embroidery projects. They work very well in Hardanger motifs.

Metal beads.

Vintage beads.

Semiprecious beads.

Metal Beads

Metal beads can be made from base metals or from precious metals such as silver or gold. They can add a rustic or royal feeling to a piece, depending on the design of the bead.

Vintage Beads

Vintage and antique beads come in all sorts of shapes and sizes. Some have two holes drilled through the beads, either in parallel directions or at right angles. They are wonderful for surface design.

Semiprecious Beads

Pearls and beads made from semiprecious stones come in all sorts of shapes and sizes.

Accent beads.

From left: Beads with center-drilled holes and beads with side-drilled holes.

Accent Beads

Large accent beads can be miniature works of art, such as these beautiful lampwork and fused glass beads. These beads work well as centerpieces, with needlework built around them.

Bead Holes

Most beads, such as seed beads and bugle beads, have a hole that goes right through the middle of the bead. But some beads, such as pressed glass leaf, flower, teardrop and other odd-shaped beads can have either a center-drilled hole or a side-drilled hole. A bead with a *side-drilled hole* means the bead hole passes through the side of the bead, usually referring to the narrow part of oval, drop, leaf or odd-shaped beads. Side-drilled holes are off center and cause the other end of the bead to hang in beadwork, which makes them great for fringes or edgings. A bead with a *center-drilled hole* means the bead hole passes through the center of the bead. You will need to consider the direction and placement of the bead hole when planning your design.

Three very different types of blue beads. Counterclockwise from left: Square-holed, silver-lined, with an aurora borealis (AB) finish; transparent beige with light blue lining; and opaque.

Bead Colors and Finishes

This is the trickiest part of all. Beads, like embroidery fibers, have different finishes and look different, depending on how shiny or dull they are and the way they are made. Shiny beads stand out, while dull beads fade into the background. The finish makes a difference, depending on the type of beadwork — whether you are using just one or two isolated beads or a large section of beads all together. Beads with an aurora borealis (AB) finish, for example, vary in color throughout the bag and will only look the same if you work them in large groups. It's a very sad thing to take a huge amount of time and effort making a project, only to find that when you step back and take a look, you've chosen a green that is too dull or a pink that fades away into the background. That is why it is very important to work up a small swatch of your project using all the materials together in similar proportions so you can see what the finished piece will look like. Beads can be tricky in the bag or tube because you are looking at all the angles of the beads together in a group. Your stitching, however, will only show the sides of the bead, and you may be stitching them in small amounts or mixed with other beads and fibers. Take the time to see how all the beads and fibers will work together before starting your project.

How Many Beads to Buy

When a set of instructions indicates the number of grams or ounces needed for the project, it is always best to buy a little more than you need, just in case you run out. Beads also have dye lots, just like yarn, and different dye lots can be very different from one another.

When purchasing beads, you may have to do a little calculating to make sure you are getting the amount you need for your project. Beads are sold in a variety of packaging including bags, tubes, little plastic boxes, by the hank or strand, or individually. When in a bag, tube or box, beads are normally measured in grams or ounces. It's not always consistent, so you sometimes need to be able to convert grams to ounces and back again to know how many beads to buy.

- 28 grams = 1 ounce
- 7 grams = ¼ ounce
- 7-gram package of size 11 seed beads = 2" square of solid embroidered beads
- Most beads are packaged in 4- to 10-gram containers.

Strands and hanks are a little more vague. A strand is a length of thread strung with beads with the thread ends tied together. A hank is two or more strands tied together. Sometimes the weight is indicated in hanks or strands, but not usually. And the length of the strands and the number of strands in a hank can vary. Weighing the beads before buying them will help determine if you have the correct amount.

A variety of containers used to store beads.

Storing Beads

Just like embroidery threads and yarn, you will need to store your beads so you can find the colors you need when you need them. You may want keep your beads in their original containers or set up your own storage system. Many beaders transfer their beads to small, clear containers (tubes or boxes) and store them by color and/or bead type. Other beaders prefer small plastic bags and organize their beads in a box or portfolio. If you move your beads to different containers, it's a good idea to transfer the bead number, if there is one, and the store where you bought it, if you buy beads from a lot of different places.

Working Containers and Surfaces for Beads

When stitching, you will need to have all the different beads you will be using out so you can easily pick them up. I use a piece of suede leather, and pour the beads into little piles. It is easy to pick them up and they don't roll and bounce away. Other surfaces and containers include bead trays, ceramic trays and dishes, thin foam padding, or, in a pinch, a kitchen dish towel (not terry cloth, you'll loose your beads in it!). You will also need a way to get the beads back into their storage containers. There are several types of bead shovels that can help you scoop up your beads to put them away.

Threads and yarn used in bead embroidery. From the upper left to the lower right: Single-strand wool yarn; Persian tapestry wool; size 5 pearl cotton; silk sewing thread; size 8 pearl cotton; size B Nymo beading thread.

Threads

Bead embroidery requires a thread that is strong enough to hold the bead in place, but is not so strong that it will rip the fabric. Some of the stitches in this book use beading thread to add beads, but most of the stitches use the same embroidery thread that was used for the stitching. Most embroideries are worked with natural fiber on cotton or linen, therefore I wouldn't use the synthetic thread, Nymo, to stitch the beads onto a fine linen wall hanging. However, if I were making a vest with a thick fabric and wanted to add beads, I might consider a strong beading thread to help the beads stay sewn on longer. If your item will be washed, look for a thread that can take the same washing as the fabric.

Recommended Threads for Bead Embroidery

For size 11 seed beads: Use two strands of six-strand embroidery floss, one strand of size 8 or size 12 pearl cotton or fine silk cord. I use beading thread for fringes and beadwork stitches sewn to fabric, but all the stitches that incorporate beads in the stitch itself use the cotton threads.

For size 8 seed beads: Use size 5 pearl cotton. This is a good size for most size 8 seed bead holes.

Common Types of Beading Threads

Nymo is a synthetic, multifilament thread that comes in several sizes and colors. Size F is thick and is used for size 8 beads. Size D is a medium thread and is used for stiff projects in size 11 beads. Size B is medium and is used for size 11 and sometimes size 15 beads. Sizes A, O and OO are thin and used for small beads.

Sylamide is a two-ply, twisted synthetic thread that is prewaxed and easy to work with. It comes in one size, which is a medium-weight beading thread.

Silk cord is a strong silk, comparable to pearl cotton in the look and use, though it has the beautiful shine of silk.

Silk thread is thin, yet strong, and is a good choice if you want a natural fiber thread when using small beads.

Common Embroidery Threads and Yarns

Six-strand embroidery floss is the traditional choice for cross-stitch on Aida cloth. It's also wonderful for bead embroidery because you can separate it into any thread combination and accommodate most bead sizes. It comes in cotton, rayon and silk.

Pearl cotton in sizes 12, 8, 5 and 3 works well for bead embroidery because it is strong and easy to work with.

Persian wool is used in needlepoint. It is a three-ply yarn that can be separated so it can be worked in several canvas sizes. You can use the wool for the needlepoint and embellish it with beads using pearl cotton or embroidery floss.

Single-strand needlepoint wool is easy to work with and shows textured stitches well, although using it with beads limits you to the larger size 8 or size 6 seed beads. You can, however, embellish stitching with beads by using a thinner thread for the beads.

Waxing Thread

In beadwork, pulling thread through beeswax or another thread conditioner strengthens it and keeps it from tangling. Do not do this in bead embroidery because it will change the sheen and character of the decorative embroidery thread and may affect the fine fabrics.

Fabrics and Canvases

Embroidery surfaces are as varied as the threads and beads used for stitching. Anything you can pull a needle and thread through can be embroidered with beads added to it. The sample stitches list the type of fabric or canvas used for the stitch displayed. The following are other fabrics and canvases used in this book.

Needlepoint

Also called canvas embroidery, this technique can be stitched on a stiff canvas with regularly spaced holes, known as mesh size, commonly from 10 to 24 stitches per inch. Traditionally, all of the canvas is covered with stitches, though that is not always the case anymore. Common types of canvas include mono, congress, Penelope, interlock and plastic canvas.

Counted Thread

Counted thread can be stitched on any fabric in which the threads or spaces between groups of threads are evenly spaced so you can count them. Common types of fabric used for counted thread embroidery include Aida, linen and Hardanger.

Pulled Thread, Drawn Work, Insertion Stitches

Pulled thread and drawn work both need to be worked on fabric similar to counted thread projects, since you need to be able to count the fabric threads to work the stitches. Pulled thread also needs to be worked on a loosely woven or lightweight fabric so you can pull the stitches tight to manipulate the fabric. Insertion stitches can be worked along any space between any fabrics that have been turned under. They also can be worked on two edges of ribbon to attach them together.

Hardanger

Hardanger is worked on Hardanger fabric or fine, even woven cotton. Hardanger fabric is a woven cotton made from thread pairs woven in an even, simple weave, making it easy to count the threads for stitching and to cut the threads in openwork.

Freeform Embroidery

Freeform embroidery can be worked on any fabric, from blue jeans to the finest silk. Patterned fabric is especially appealing to use since you can incorporate the pattern into the stitching design.

Crazy Quilt Stitches

Crazy quilt stitches, traditionally worked on scrap quilts often using fine satins and velvets, can be worked on any fabric.

Smocking

Smocking is usually worked on thin-weight cottons or gingham because they are easy to gather for smocking. Smocking, however, can be worked on thicker fabrics, too.

Ribbonwork

Ribbonwork can be worked on most types of fabrics, though more loosely woven and/or thinner fabrics are easier to pull stitches through.

Beading Stitches

Beading stitches can be worked on most fabrics, from cottons to canvas. When working with canvas, experiment until you get the correct number of beads in relation to the holes in the canvas.

Fringes and Edgings

Fringes and edgings can be worked on just about any fabric. Edgings are especially useful in finishing off edges of needlework.

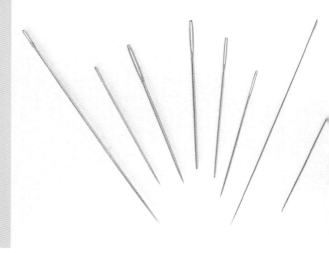

Needles for bead embroidery. From left: Size 7 gold eye basting; size 9 crewel; size 24 chenille; sizes 24, 26 and 28 tapestry; size 10 beading; size 10 bead embroidery.

Needles

Needles are an important part of beadwork. You want the biggest needle you can get so you can thread and work with it easily, but it has to be small enough to get through those little bead holes. Beads require thinner needles and threads than some embroidery fibers.

Beading Needles

The bead embroidery needle on the far right of the photo has a blunt end, while the longer beading needle next to it has a sharp end. Both needles are great for stringing beads, but the small eyes only work with the smaller threads.

Tapestry Needles

Tapestry needles have long, large eyes and blunt ends. The size 28 needle works with size 11 seed beads, and sizes 26 and 24 work well with size 8 beads. These needles accommodate larger threads than the beading needles, but are thin enough to pick up the beads. Therefore, they work well for all of the charted patterns.

Chenille

Chenille needles look the same as tapestry needles (long, large eyes), but they have a sharp point. These, like the crewel needles, are good needles for noncharted embroidery that requires piercing the fabric rather than passing between the threads of the fabric. Because of the large eyes, they are ideal for ribbon embroidery.

Crewel

Crewel needles have a sharp point and a larger eye than the beading needles. They work well with size 8 seed beads for the techniques that require piercing the fabric, such as freeform embroidery, crazy quilt stitching and smocking. With patience, you can coax size 8 pearl cotton through them and use them with size 11 seed beads as well.

Gold Eye Basting

This basting needle is strong, long and not too thick. It, like the crewel needle, works well with size 8 seed beads on non-charted embroidery.

Incidentals

In addition to your beads, threads, fabric and needles, you will need to have several other tools handy.

Scissors

In addition to basic sewing scissors for cutting your fabric, you will also need some small, sharp scissors for cutting threads.

Laying Tools

If you are stitching with multiple threads, you may want to use a laying tool to help arrange the threads parallel to each other as you pull them into place. You can also use your fingers or needle for this purpose.

Threaders and Thimbles

These come in handy for a variety of stitching projects, helping you to keep from straining your eyes and to protect your fingers from sharp needles.

Hoops and Frames

Stitching large projects is much easier when they are stretched on a frame. Smaller projects can be easier when they are in a small hoop.

Lighting and Magnification

Be sure to take care of your eyes by always having adequate lighting and by using amplification tools like reading glasses or magnifying lamps so you don't strain your eyes.

Rulers, Pencils and Measuring Tapes

At some point in most projects, these will come in handy, whether it is to plan your design placement at the beginning of the project, or to help plan in the framing or finishing. For freeform embroidery and crazy quilt embroidery, you may want to draw the main points of the design directly onto the fabric, lightly in pencil.

Basic Techniques

Preparing the Fabric

You will need to prepare most fabrics for bead embroidery by pressing them to remove any wrinkles or creases, and then stretching the fabric on a stretcher frame or placing it in a hoop so you have a taut surface for your stitching. This is especially important if you have a design in which the embroidery is spaced more than 1" apart, since you will need to carry loose thread behind your work. The stretched fabric will ensure that the loose thread isn't pulled too tight, which can cause puckering in your finished piece.

Threading the Needle

Yarn and textured fibers are sometimes difficult to thread because the soft, fuzzy fibers won't all go through the eye of the needle at the same time. The easiest way to thread your needle with these fibers is to fold the tail of yarn over the needle and pinch it firmly with your thumb and pointer finger. Then

slide the needle out from between your fingers and pass the needle's eye down between your thumb and pointer finger so that you are pushing the needle's eye onto the pinched and folded yarn. Once the fold goes through the eye, then you can unpinch the yarn and pull it all the way through the eye.

Pearl cotton is often too thick to get through the needle once you've folded it in half, especially when using a thin needle to string beads. With pearl cotton, you need to wet the end of the thread, pinch it flat, then cut the end with sharp scissors and pinch it flat again between your thumb and pointer finger. Slide the needle between your fingers onto the cut thread. It may only go through a little bit, and then you will need to carefully pull it through, leaving a 2" tail.

Starting and Ending the Thread

One of the easiest ways to start your embroidery is to tie a large knot at the very end of the thread or yarn and pass the needle into the fabric or canvas from the front side of the work about 3" from your stitching area, away from the stitches you will be working. Then, after you finish stitching, you can cut the knot, pass the tail to the back side of the work, then thread it with a needle and weave it into your finished embroidery.

Another method is to thread your needle and pass

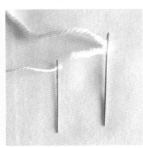

The needle on the left shows how to thread a needle with pearl cotton, and the needle on the right shows how to thread a needle with yarn.

"Knot on the right side" method.

the needle up at the beginning of your embroidery from the back side of your work, pulling the thread or yarn until there is about 1" to 2" of tail left. Then, catch the tail in the first stitches you make in your embroidery.

Stitching Methods

There are two ways to make stitches. The one on the right in the photo is called the stabbing method.

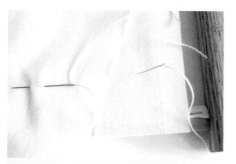

Sewing (left) and stabbing (right) methods of stitching.

To end your thread or yarn, pass the needle through some of the stitches on the back side of the needle work. If the stitches are loose, pass the needle back in the other direction as well. Cut the thread or yarn close to the stitches.

This is when you pass the needle from the front to the back of the fabric, pull the stitch into place, then pass the needle back up through the fabric for the next stitch and pull it through. The other way is the sewing method. Simply push the needle in and out of the fabric and then pull it through so that the needle is always coming out on the top side of the fabric. The stabbing method works well for needlepoint and counted thread embroidery because the completed stitches are more uniform. It is also easier to work when your project is in a hoop or frame. The other method is good for stitches such as chain stitch and buttonhole or blanket stitch, where you need to catch a loop of the thread as you pull the thread through. It is usually worked without a hoop or frame, though you can work it on a frame or hoop if you don't have the fabric pulled very tightly.

Reading the Charts and Diagrams

Each stitch in The Stitches section is accompanied by a chart or diagram showing how to make the stitch. The examples below point out what the symbols mean in the charts and diagrams.

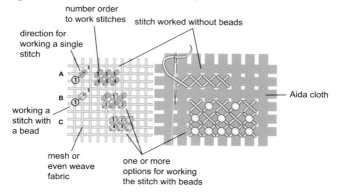

number order to work stitches

stitch worked without beads

direction for working a single stitch

A

B

working a stitch with a bead   C

Aida cloth

mesh or even weave fabric

one or more options for working the stitch with beads

Section 2: The Stitches

The following stitch samples are arranged by stitch type, showing first the stitch without beads and then one or more ways to add beads to the stitch, except for the last three sections which are only worked with beads. Each stitch section states the type and size of beads, needles, thread and fabric used for the sample so you can easily duplicate the stitch as shown. An illustration of the steps to make the stitch is accompanied by notes on how the beads were added in the examples. (Refer back to page 47 for additional information on reading the illustration charts/diagrams, if necessary.) Some stitches can simply be replaced by beads, or modified so beads can be a part of the stitch. Others can only be embellished with beads sewn over the completed stitch. These examples show just a few of the many ways to work beads into embroidery stitches.

Needlepoint

Adding beads to needlepoint is a little different than adding beads to the other embroidery stitches, since many needlepoint projects are worked in thick yarn, rather than thread. Because of this, you have the choice between adding beads after completing your needlepoint project, stitching them on top of the needlepoint stitches, or adding the beads into the needlepoint pattern. If you add the beads into the needlepoint pattern stitch, you will usually need to work the yarn part of the pattern first, then add the bead-filled stitches afterwards, using a thinner needle and thread. All of the samples in this section were worked on 10-count mono canvas, using single-strand tapestry yarn and size 11 or size 8 seed beads with size 8 or 12 pearl cotton. The yarn was stitched with a size 20 tapestry needle and the beads were stitched with a size 28 tapestry needle, or a beading needle for the size 11 beads, and a size 28 or size 24 tapestry needle for the size 8 beads.

1 Tent

Also known as half cross, basketweave and continental.

Skill Level: Easy

Description: This is the simplest and smallest diagonal stitch. It can be worked in any direction. When worked diagonally, it is called *basketweave stitch*. This is considered the best form of the stitch because it produces an even looking stitch that doesn't pull the canvas on the bias and covers the back of the canvas completely, making it very durable. When moving from stitch to stitch horizontally so that the next stitch is begun in the opposite side of the direction of the stitching, it is called *continental stitch*, which is the next best method because it covers the back of the canvas and is long wearing. Finally, when making the stitch and beginning the next stitch directly to the right, creating a small vertical stitch on the back of the canvas, it is called *half cross stitch*, which is the least favored because it is often uneven and is short wearing because of the lack of coverage on the back of the canvas.

Beads: This stitch is ideal for single beads that are the same size as the stitch, or it can be used with more than one bead for a raised texture.

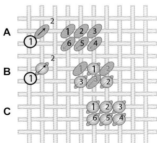

Here's How: Come up at (1), string one bead, pass over one thread intersection diagonally and pass into fabric at (2).

2 Cross

Skill Level: Easy

Description: This stitch is made of one diagonal stitch with another stitch worked in the opposite direction, crossing over it. It can be worked as shown, or each cross can be completed individually before moving on. Work it over any number of canvas threads.

Beads: Add beads to the stitches as they are made as shown in example C, or added between stitches as in B. Example D shows how to work the bottom stitch with two beads and the top with three beads. The beads fit snugly together in this arrangement.

Here's How: Example D: Come up at (1), string two beads, pass diagonally over two thread intersections and enter fabric at (2). Repeat across row. Stitching in the opposite direction, bring needle up at (7), string three beads and pass down at (8), making sure the two beads from the first half of the stitch stay on either side of the second half as you finish. Repeat across the row.

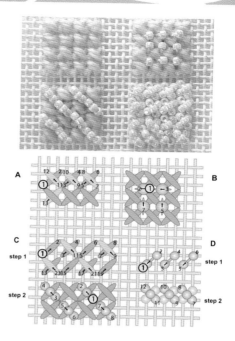

3 St. George's Cross

Also known as upright cross.

Skill Level: Easy

Description: It is made of equal-length vertical and horizontal stitches that form an upright cross. Work over two stitches in rows that begin one canvas thread over from the previous row.

Beads: Shown here is a vertical beaded stitch in place of every other row. When adding beads to some pattern stitches, alter the stitch as you go.

Here's How: Come up at (1), down at (2), up at (3) and down at (4). Skip one thread space to the right and repeat the pattern across the row. To add a bead in the next row, begin in one thread below the completed stitches, stitching over the skipped spaces, come up at (1), as in example B, string one bead and pass down at (2). Skip one thread space

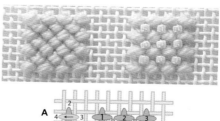

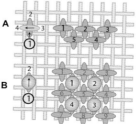

to the right and repeat the beaded stitch. Alternate one row with beads and one without.

4 Long Upright Cross

Skill Level: Easy

Description: An elongated version of #3 St. George's Cross, this stitch is worked over two vertical threads and four horizontal threads.

Beads: It is possible to add beads to the long or the short sections of this stitch. This example shows the long stitches worked with yarn first, then the short stitches worked using pearl cotton. A bead was added on every other stitch.

Here's How: Come up at (1), down at (2), up at (3), string one bead and pass down at (4). Skip one thread space to the right and repeat the stitch pattern across the row. Repeat the same stitch pattern in the skipped spaces for the next row.

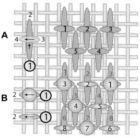

5 Fern

Skill Level: Intermediate

Description: This stitch is made of equal-sized diagonal overlapping stitches, creating columns of raised texture. This stitch is always worked from top to bottom.

Beads: Because this stitch is so dense, instead of working the beads in the actual stitches, leave a column of canvas free, then add a column of beads with a horizontal stitch between the fern stitches.

Here's How: Come up at (1), down at (2), up at (3) and down at (4). Come up one space below (1) and repeat the stitch, working vertically. Skip a space and repeat the stitch, creating another vertical line of stitches. For the bead pattern, fill in the skipped spaces by bringing the needle up at (1) as shown in B, stringing one bead, then passing back down at (2). Bring the needle back up one space below (1) and repeat, working vertically.

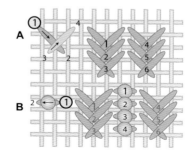

6 Van Dyke

Skill Level: Intermediate

Description: These overlapping, elongated cross stitches are worked from top to bottom as in fern stitch, creating a dense herringbone pattern.

Beads: Add the beads to the completed Van Dyke stitch with alternating half cross stitches that fit into the lower sections of the stitch.

Here's How: Come up at (1), down at (2), up at (3) and down at (4). Come up two spaces below (1) and repeat the stitch, working vertically. For the next row, begin at the top of the row, bringing the needle up one space above (4) in the first stitch, then repeat the stitch pattern, working down vertically. For the bead pattern, bring the needle up at (1), as shown in B, stringing one bead and passing down at (2). Bring the needle up at (3), string one bead and pass down at (4). Repeat the stitch, working vertically.

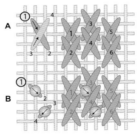

7 Slanting Gobelin

Also known as oblique gobelin.

Skill Level: Easy

Description: This stitch consists of straight stitches worked over one vertical stitch by two or more horizontal stitches.

Beads: Because this stitch is so simple, there are many possibilities for beads. Example B shows the finished stitch with backstitches of beads added in a three-stitch pattern, while example C shows every other stitch of the pattern filled with beads.

Here's How: Demonstrating C: Come up at (1), string three beads and pass down at (2). Alternate one stitch with beads and one without.

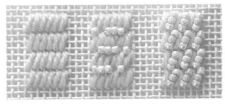

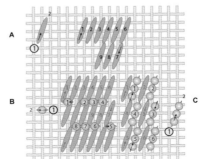

8 Upright Gobelin

Also known as straight gobelin.

Skill Level: Easy

Description: Work vertical stitches over any number of horizontal canvas threads, usually up to six.

Beads: Example B shows size 11 beads worked in backstitch between two rows of upright gobelin stitch, while example C shows the size 8 beads filling every other stitch in the pattern. To achieve the look in example C, first work with the yarn, skipping one canvas thread, then go back with the beads and pearl cotton.

Here's How: Demonstrating C: Come up at (1), string three beads and pass down at (2). Alternate one stitch with beads and one without.

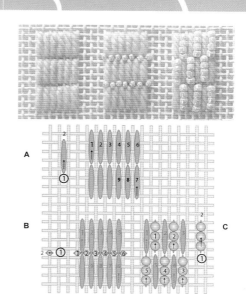

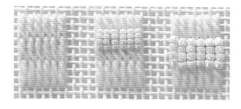

9 Split Upright Gobelin

Also known as split stitch.

Skill Level: Easy

Description: The same as #8 Upright Gobelin, except in each following row, the stitches overlap the row above, splitting the stitch.

Beads: Example B shows size 11 beads worked over the finished stitch. Add beads between rows by coming up two canvas threads below the top of the second row and going down two canvas threads above the bottom of the first row, splitting both rows. Example C shows beads added to a modified stitch. For this look, make two rows of upright gobelin, skipping two horizontal canvas threads between rows. Fill gap with size 8 beads and pearl cotton, over four horizontal threads, splitting both rows of yarn as you stitch.

Here's How: Example C: Come up at (1), string four beads and enter at (2). Stitch every other row without beads first and then add rows with beads.

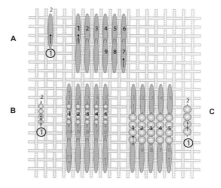

10 Encroaching Upright Gobelin

Also known as interlocking gobelin.

Skill Level: Easy

Description: This stitch is the same as #9 Split Upright Gobelin, but instead of splitting the yarn in the previous row, enter the canvas on one side of the yarn, always on the same side for each stitch. This creates a slight slant to the finished pattern.

Beads: Example B shows beads added to the finished stitch. Come up between two stitches at the center of the stitches, string three beads and pass under the stitch in the next row. String three beads and pass through the stitch in the next row below. In this method, only enter the canvas at the beginning and end of the bead pattern. Example C shows the beads added as a part of the stitch in a row. Either work the yarn rows first and then the bead rows, or work one yarn row and then one bead row.

Here's How: Example C: Come up at (1), string

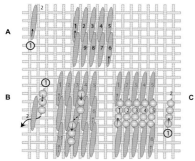

four beads and pass down at (2). Alternate one row with beads and one row without beads.

11 Interlocking Upright Gobelin

Also known as interlocking straight gobelin.

Skill Level: Easy

Description: This stitch is the same as #10 Encroaching Upright Gobelin, except enter the stitch on the opposite side of the previous row. In this stitch, the pattern retains its vertical structure.

Beads: Example B: Backstitch three size 11 beads over one row of the finished stitch, working in a wave across canvas. Example C: Use size 11 beads as the middle row of the stitch. The yarn rows can be worked separately before the bead rows, or work one yarn row and one bead row and repeat the pattern.

Here's How: Example C: Come up at (1), string five beads and enter at (2). Alternate one row with beads and one without.

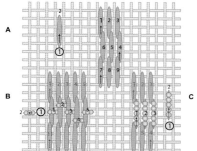

12 Cashmere

Skill Level: Intermediate

Description: This is a basic rectangle made from two long diagonal stitches bordered by two short diagonal stitches. Though easy to stitch, be careful to use the same tension for the short stitches as for the long stitches.

Beads: This example replaces the short stitches with beads. First, complete the long stitches, then go back and add the short stitches with the size 8 beads and pearl cotton.

Here's How: Come up at (1), down at (2), up at (3), down at (4), up at (5), down at (6), up at (7) and down at (8). Repeat, working horizontally to the left, beginning the next stitch group by coming up one space to the left of (3).

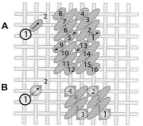

13 Framed Cashmere

Skill Level: Intermediate

Description: By leaving a canvas thread between the cashmere blocks, you can then fill in the spaces with tent stitch. This technique can be used on any stitches that are made of blocks, such as Scotch, mosaic or cross stitch.

Beads: This example shows the tent stitches replaced with size 8 beads using pearl cotton. Another option is to reverse the design, working the cashmere stitches in beads and working the tent stitch in yarn.

Here's How: Stitch one Cashmere block, as in #12 Cashmere, then begin the next block two spaces over to the left, so each block is surrounded by one canvas thread. Line up the blocks in rows and columns separated by one thread in the canvas. Fill in the spaces with beaded tent stitches (#1 Tent) by bringing the needle up at (1) as shown in B, stringing one bead and passing over one thread intersection diagonally and into the fabric at (2).

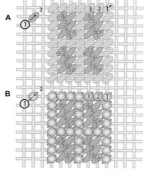

14 Cashmere Checker

Skill Level: Intermediate

Description: Here, the cashmere blocks are alternated with tent stitches, creating a checkered pattern. This technique can be used on any stitches that are made of blocks, such as Scotch, mosaic or cross stitch.

Beads: The size 8 beads used for the tent stitches accentuate the checker pattern.

Here's How: Stitch #12 Cashmere blocks, alternating with two-stitch by three-stitch beaded blocks of #1 Tent stitch as follows: Come up one space to the left of the first long stitch in the cashmere block, string one bead, pass diagonally over one intersection of canvas threads and into the canvas. Repeat the beaded tent stitch two times above the first stitch and one stitch to the left of the three stitches.

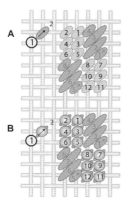

15 Reversed Cashmere

Skill Level: Intermediate

Description: Unlike other cashmere stitches with a right-slanting stitch pattern, alternately reverse the stitch direction here to create a subtle pattern change. Use on any stitches that are made of blocks, such as Scotch, mosaic or cross stitch.

Beads: This is the same bead technique shown in the basic #12 Cashmere stitch where the beads were used for the short stitches, but notice the new effect.

Here's How: Stitch two long #12 Cashmere stitches and then bring needle up at the base of the second stitch and down two spaces up and two spaces to the left. Make the same stitch one space below. Repeat the four-stitch repeat across row and reverse for each row below. To add beaded #1 Tent stitches, bring needle up one space to right of first long stitch, string one bead and pass diagonally over intersection of two threads and into fabric. Repeat at each intersection of canvas threads above and below each long-stitch group.

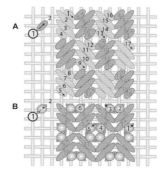

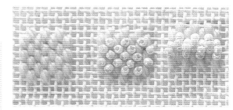

16 Diagonal Cashmere

Skill Level: Intermediate

Description: Stitch pattern diagonally with two long stitches, then one short stitch. Repeat in a descending diagonal line. Fit next row into first with short stitch lining up diagonally with second long stitch.

Beads: Use the same technique as the basic #12 Cashmere stitch, simply replacing short stitches with size 8 beads and pearl cotton. Notice the very different finished look.

Here's How: Come up and pass over two canvas thread intersections up and to the right and then into canvas. Make another stitch one space below. Skip over one canvas thread intersection down and to the right and come up through the space. Repeat two-stitch pattern. To add beaded #1 Tent stitches, come up one space above first long stitch, string one bead and pass diagonally over one canvas thread intersection and back into fabric. Repeat beaded tent stitch one space to the right of the second long stitch in every pattern repeat.

17 Brick

Also known as alternating.

Skill Level: Easy

Description: Stitch consists of simple vertical stitches worked over two horizontal canvas threads. Every other stitch in a row is offset by one thread.

Beads: Example below incorporates a row of beads in the stitch pattern by using three size 8 beads and pearl cotton for one row to create raised pattern across the row. Example on right: Add size 8 beads at base of each stitch after the yarn pattern is done. Because the pearl cotton comes in and out of the same hole for each bead, the beads tilt randomly over the stitching.

Here's How: Example on right: Come up at (1) and down at (2). Come up one space diagonally down and to the right of (1) and down two spaces up. Make the next vertical stitch one space to the right and aligned with the first stitch and the next stitch one space to the right and aligned with the second stitch. Repeat across with each row in the same pattern. To add beads, bring needle up between two vertical stitches, string one bead and pass down in same space. Repeat across between each row.

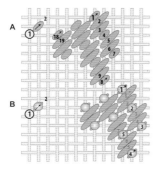

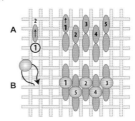

18 Parisian

Skill Level: Intermediate

Description: This long-and-short vertical stitch pattern is worked over two and four canvas threads across the row. Stitch successive rows with short stitches below long stitches and long stitches below short stitches of the previous row.

Beads: Use three size 8 beads in place of short stitches.

Here's How: Come up at (1), string three beads and pass down at (2), creating a short vertical beaded stitch. Come up one space diagonally down and to right of (1) and down one space diagonally up and to right of (2), creating a long vertical stitch. Repeat two-stitch pattern across row. Make successive rows so beaded stitches are below long stitches.

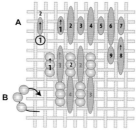

19 Hungarian

Skill Level: Intermediate

Description: Three vertical stitches over two, four and two canvas threads create diamond pattern. Work each diamond with a space between, which is filled with the diamond row below and offset. Short stitches fall in vertical line, as do the long stitches.

Beads: Stitch three size 11 beads onto finished pattern from point to point of the long stitches. Add size 8 beads at the intersections of beads in bottom row.

Here's How: Come up at (1) and down at (2), creating a short vertical stitch. Come up one space diagonally down and to right of (1) and down one space diagonally up and to right of (2), creating a long vertical stitch. Make another short stitch next to the long stitch aligned with the first short stitch. Skip one space and make the same three-stitch pattern to the right. Repeat across row. On next row, line up short stitches and long stitches vertically under the previous row. To add beaded stitches, come up one space to the left of the center of first stitch in first row, string three beads

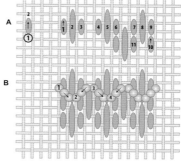

and pass down at the base of the first long stitch. Come up at the top of the long stitch in next row below, string three beads and pass down at the base of first long stitch. Repeat zigzag pattern across and between rows.

20 Pavilion

Also known as Hungarian diamonds.

Skill Level: Intermediate

Description: Make a diamond of three graduated vertical stitches bordered by one short stitch.

Beads: Use size 11 beads backstitched horizontally over two vertical canvas threads between every longest and shortest stitch.

Here's How: Come up at (1) and down at (2), creating short stitch. Come up one space diagonally down and to right of (1) and down one space diagonally up and to right of (2), creating long stitch. Make another long stitch one space longer on top and bottom, make one the same size as the second and then one the same size as the first, creating a diamond. Repeat across, omitting first short stitch in the repeat. Fit each following row so longest stitches line up vertically with shortest stitches of previous row. To add beaded stitches, come up one space to the left of the intersection of shortest and longest stitches, string one bead and

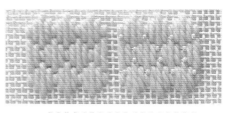

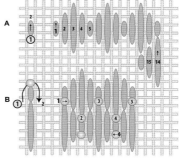

pass down one space to the right of intersection. Repeat at each intersection.

21 Beaty

Skill Level: Easy

Description: Each row alternates two short stitches and two long stitches, both beginning at the same horizontal canvas thread. The next row is the opposite-length stitch from the one above.

Beads: Backstitch size 11 beads over the center vertical canvas thread between each pair of same-length stitches. Stitch three beads for picot effect.

Here's How: Come up at (1), down at (2) and repeat one space to right. Come up one space to right and two spaces up and pass down two spaces up, aligned with top of other stitches. Make same short stitch one space to the right. Repeat pattern across row. Make next row so short stitches are below long ones and line up across bottom of the row. For beaded stitches, come up at base of second-to-last stitch at right end of row, string three beads and pass down one space to the right. Come up at base of fourth stitch from end, string three beads

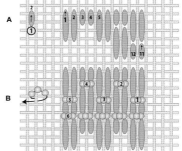

and pass down one space to right. Repeat for each set of two stitches across each row.

22 Wild Goose Chase

Skill Level: Intermediate

Description: Create stitch's slanting rectangle by repeating four graduated vertical stitches across row and then repeating in reverse order back.

Beads: Example B: Stem stitch seven size 11 beads, making a stitch in every other vertical canvas thread at base of horizontal line made from two rows of pattern.

Here's How: Come up at (1), down at (2), up at (3), down at (4), up at (5), down at (6), up at (7) and down at (8). Repeat horizontally to right. On next row, come up one space below last long stitch and make graduated stitches line up along bottom edges, working to the left. On next row, stitch a mirror image of previous row and have stitches fill spaces below previous row and line up along bottom. To add beads, come up one space left of the intersection of two rows that line up horizontally, string three beads, pass down two spaces to right and come up one space to left. Repeat across the row.

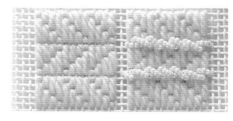

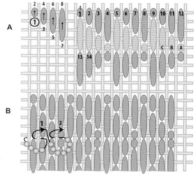

23 Milanese

Skill Level: Intermediate

Description: Triangles stitched in diagonal rows make up this stitch. Begin with small half cross, increase length of stitch successively and repeat again, working diagonally down and to the right. Repeat in the opposite direction for the next row.

Beads: Use a size 8 bead to replace smallest stitch in the repeat on one row. Work all yarn stitches first, leaving the smallest stitch unworked. Then go back and fill in with the beads and pearl cotton.

Here's How: Come up at (1), down at (2), up at (3), down at (4), up at (5), down at (6), up at (7) and down at (8). Repeat, working diagonally down and to the right. Stitch next row, reversing the direction of triangle shapes and skipping the smallest stitch in each triangle-shaped repeat. To add beads, go back and add the smallest stitch, stringing one bead before completing each stitch.

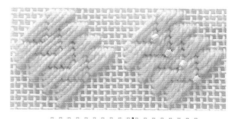

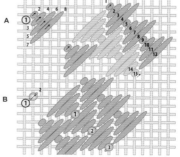

24 Roman II

Skill Level: Easy

Description: This woven-looking pattern is made of offset pairs of vertical stitches with horizontal stitches at the base of each pair of stitches.

Beads: Diagonal beaded lines change the look. Come up at base of the right vertical stitch in a pair of stitches. String two size 8 beads and pass under the next horizontal stitch to the left. Repeat across pattern and end by entering canvas at top of the right vertical stitch in the next pair to the left.

Here's How: Come up at (1), down at (2), up at (3), down at (4), up at (5), down at (6), up at (7) and down at (8). Repeat across row and in opposite direction for next row. For horizontal stitches, come up at (9), down at (10), up at (11) and down at (12), repeating across all vertical stitches. To add beads, come up at (2), exit below horizontal stitch, string two beads and pass under next horizontal stitch down and to the right. Repeat to end of pattern and enter fabric under last horizontal stitch. Repeat in diagonal rows.

25 Pavilion Steps

Skill Level: Intermediate

Description: Horizontally stitched rows of diamonds are bordered by vertically stitched zigzag stripes. Use three colors to resemble patchwork's traditional tumbling blocks pattern.

Beads: Backstitch six size 11 beads from diamond point to point, accentuating two stitch directions.

Here's How: Come up and pass vertically over four canvas threads and go back down. Make three stitches, beginning each one space above to the right. Make three stitches, beginning each one space down to the right. Repeat across the row. Make next row in opposite direction to create diamond opening. Fill opening with horizontal stitches. To add beads, come up at top of diamond, string six beads, pass down at left end of longest horizontal stitch, come up at diamond top again, string six beads and pass down at right end of longest horizontal stitch. Repeat along edges of all diamonds.

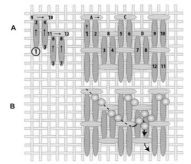

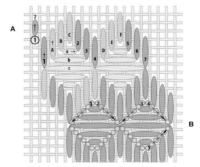

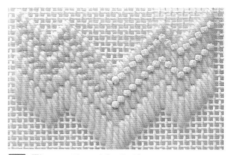

26 Florentine

Also known as bargello.

Skill Level: Intermediate

Description: Vertical stitches, usually the same length across each row, stitched in changing diagonal and wavy lines, create a flowing pattern. Subsequent rows usually follow path of first row.

Beads: Backstitch size 8 beads between rows after stitching is done.

Here's How: Come up, pass vertically over four canvas threads and back down. Make two same-sized stitches next to the first, two one space down and two more two spaces down, continuing across row as in graph. Repeat for second row. Make third row over two canvas threads and the last row over three canvas threads. To add beads, come up at bottom of last stitch in second row, string one bead and pass down one space to right above. Come up at bottom of next stitch to left and backstitch across bottom of second row. Pass through beads again to line up in a smooth curve.

27 Florentine Variation

Skill Level: Intermediate

Description: Same as #26 Florentine, except the step from stitch to stitch follows a straight line.

Beads: Use size 8 beads in place of rows.

Here's How: Come up at (1), down at (2) and up one space above to right. Make eight more vertical stitches, stepping up one space for each. Make three stitches, stepping one space down for each. Make five stitches, stepping up one space for each. Come up four spaces down from first stitch and repeat row 1, but over three threads and with one thread space between rows. Come up four spaces down from first stitch in second row and stitch next row over three threads. Come up five spaces down from first stitch in third row and stitch next row over five threads. To add beads, come up at top of first stitch in second row, string one bead and pass down one space above. Repeat across top of second and third rows.

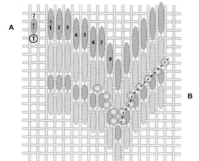

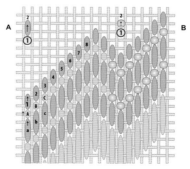

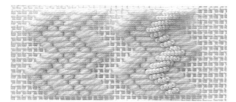

28 Medieval Mosaic

Skill Level: Intermediate

Description: Almost a modified version of #26 Florentine, this stitch is worked with horizontal stitches in an eight-stitch zigzag repeat.

Beads: Stitch four size 11 beads over yarn pattern for short stitches and seven for long stitches.

Here's How: Come up at (1) and down at (2). Repeat three more stitches, offset one space to left. Make a long horizontal stitch over four threads, beginning one space to the left and below last short stitch. Stitch three long stitches, offset by one space to the right. Make a short stitch centered under last long stitch. Make three short stitches and one long stitch, offset one space up to the left. Make three long stitches, offset to the right. Repeat pattern. To add beads, come up at end of top long stitch in the second column, so needle exits below the stitch but through same hole. String seven beads and pass down at other end of stitch, entering the hole above the stitch but in the same hole. Repeat, using four beads for the short stitches.

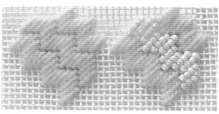

29 Byzantine

Skill Level: Intermediate

Description: Work this pattern of diagonal stitches with all stitches and rows the same length, or with varied stitch thicknesses for each row.

Beads: Replace a row of stitching with size 8 beads. Because beads are thicker than yarn, use three strands of beads for each step, rather than the four strands used in the yarn pattern. You may need to skip a stitch before or after a turn. If beads don't fit the space, make adjustments that aren't always a regular repeat.

Here's How: Come up and pass down diagonally up to the right into third space in fabric. Make another diagonal stitch below the first and three to the right of second stitch and then three below the last stitch. Repeat pattern. To add beads, come up three spaces diagonally down and left of the first stitch. String four beads and pass down at base of first stitch. Repeat same pattern as first row, adding four beads to each stitch, making only enough stitches to fit width of the beads.

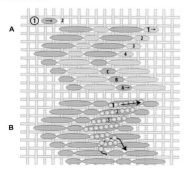

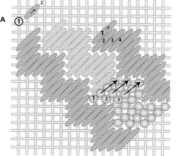

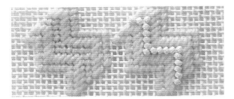

30 Jacquard

Skill Level: Intermediate

Description: This stitch is a variation of #29 Byzantine made of a stair-step pattern of diagonal stitches bordered by #1 Tent stitches.

Beads: Simply replacing the tent stitches with size 8 beads accentuates the pattern.

Here's How: Come up through canvas, pass diagonally up to the right one space and into fabric. Make another five diagonal stitches to the right of the first and then five below the last stitch. Repeat the 10-stitch pattern. Begin the next row two spaces diagonally down to the left and stitch the same pattern, making the stitches over two canvas intersections instead of one. For the beaded row, bring needle up one space diagonally below and left of the first long stitch, string a bead and pass into fabric at base of long stitch. Follow the same pattern as the other rows, adding a bead to each stitch. Stitch another long stitch row, then a short stitch row.

31 Oriental

Skill Level: Intermediate

Description: Make #23 Milanese rows, bordered by vertical stitches. Work in one color for a diagonal herringbone pattern or use two or more colors for a completely different stripe.

Beads: Replace the smallest stitch with three size 8 beads to add texture to the design.

Here's How: Come up and go down through third space above. Make another vertical stitch, beginning one space below and ending one space above previous stitch. Repeat pattern across row, stitching left to right and skipping one space between each pair of stitches. Come up two spaces down and one space to the left of the bottom of first stitch and pass down three spaces above. Make two more vertical stitches the same size, offset by one space lower and to the right. Repeat pattern across row. Repeat first two rows in the opposite direction. To add beads, come up at top of first stitch in second row, string three beads and pass down two spaces above. Repeat in every skipped space in first row.

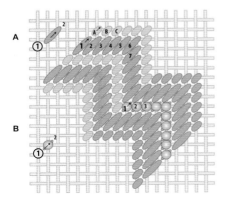

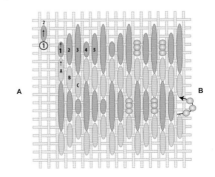

32 Scotch

Skill Level: Easy

Description: Made of five diagonal stitches, these little blocks can be stitched in the same variations used for the cashmere stitches (#12 to #16).

Beads: Add one size 8 bead in each corner of the pattern by making a half cross with a bead in the opposite direction of the yarn stitches.

Here's How: Come up and then down through next space diagonally up to right. Come up one space left of beginning of first stitch and down one space to above top of first stitch. Come up one space left of beginning of second stitch and down one space above top of second stitch. Come up one space above base of third stitch and down one space left of top of third stitch. Come up one space above base of fourth stitch and down one space left of top of fourth stitch. Repeat five-stitch squares in rows, turning canvas for each row. To add beads, come up between the smallest and next-sized stitch, pass under smallest stitch, string one bead, pass under smallest stitch in next block diagonally and pass down between smallest and next-sized stitch. Repeat at each block intersection.

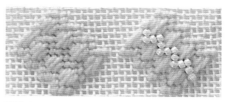

33 Moorish

Skill Level: Intermediate

Description: This stitch is a composite of diagonal Scotch stitch bordered with tent stitch.

Beads: The example shows the center row of tent stitch, replaced with size 8 beads.

Here's How: Come up through canvas and down through next space diagonally up to right. Come up one space below beginning of first stitch and down one space to right of top of first stitch. Come up one space below start of second stitch and down one space to right of top of second stitch. Come up one space to right of base of third stitch and down one space below top of third stitch. Come up one space to right of base of fourth stitch and down one space below top of fourth stitch. Repeat from second stitch, making a diagonal zigzag pattern. Stitch #1 Tent along top side of pattern. To add beads, come up one space diagonally down and left of first stitch, string one bead, pass down at base of first stitch. Repeat at base of all stitches along the pattern.

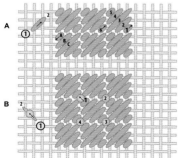

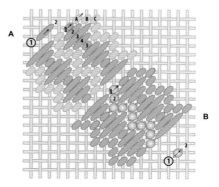

34 Oblique Slav

Also known as wide gobelin.

Skill Level: Easy

Description: This stitch is a very slanted gobelin stitch that is worked in every other stitch across four canvas threads and up two canvas threads.

Beads: Complete the stitch and add size 8 beads by working vertically, passing under the stitch above, stringing a bead, and passing under the next stitch above. The only place the pearl cotton enters the canvas is at the beginning and end of the row.

Here's How: Come up at (1) and down at (2). Come up two spaces right of (1). Repeat same stitch across, spacing each stitch two spaces apart. Begin next row by coming up two spaces below (1). Repeat across row. To add beads, come up one space above and to right of base of second stitch in first row, string one bead, pass under second stitch in second row. Repeat for each row. Pass needle into fabric at second space right of second stitch in last row.

35 Kalem

Also known as kelim, knit or knitting.

Skill Level: Intermediate

Description: These columns of diagonal stitches reverse direction every column, creating a pattern that resembles stockinette stitch in knitwear.

Beads: In example B above, the finished pattern is embellished with three size 11 beads worked over the stitch in the same pattern technique. In example C above, the stitch is worked completely in beads, using three size 11 beads for each stitch.

Here's How: Example B: Come up through canvas, pass down one space above. Come up one space below base of first stitch and down one space left of top of first stitch. Repeat the second stitch in a column with each stitch one space apart. For next column, come up at base of last stitch and down two spaces to right of top of last stitch. Working up, repeat same stitch in a column. Make three pairs of columns. To add beads, repeat same stitch over the center column, adding three beads to each stitch.

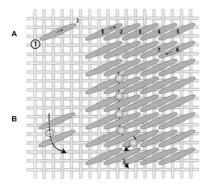

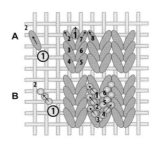

36 Stem

Skill Level: Intermediate

Description: Unlike stem stitch in freeform embroidery, this needlepoint stem stitch is a combination of half cross stitches worked vertically that reverse direction from column to column, and with a small vertical stitch between each V-shape.

Beads: Use beads in place of the small vertical stitch. Notice how the beads slant differently from one column to the next. Work the first column top to bottom and the second bottom to top.

Here's How: Come up at (1), down at (2), up at (3), down at (4). Come up one space below (1) and repeat two-stitch pattern in a column. To add beads, begin at top of the column and come up at (5), string one bead and pass down one space above. Come up one space below (5) and repeat stitch down column.

37 Leaf

Skill Level: Intermediate

Description: Opposing diagonal stitches taper to one vertical stitch at the top, creating a leaf. Vary number of stitches per section to change pattern.

Beads: Add a vein with seven size 11 beads or work the whole leaf in beads. The all-bead leaf was worked with five beads in the vertical stitch, six in the two stitches on either side of first stitch, seven in next two stitches and eight in each of last six.

Here's How: Leaf with bead vein: Come up at (1), down at (2), up three spaces right and four spaces up from (2), down at (2). Repeat stitch pair twice in next spaces above. Come up one space diagonally up and to right of beginning of last left stitch and go down one stitch above base of last stitches. Come up four stitches right of top of last stitch and go down one stitch above base of last stitch. Come up one space diagonally up and left of the top of last right stitch and go down at base of last stitch. Come up two stitches left of top of last stitch and go down at base of last stitch. Come up five stitches above base of last stitch and go down

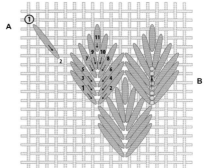

three stitches below. To add beads, come up at base of first two stitches, string seven or eight beads and pass down at base of last slanting pair of stitches.

Counted Thread

Counted thread and needlepoint have always meshed somewhat, with many projects pulling from both techniques. Most, if not all, of the needlepoint stitches above can be used for counted thread projects. Here is a small sampling of counted thread stitches showing their appearance on a counted thread fabric. The samples in this section were made using 14-count Aida cloth, size 8 pearl cotton, a bead embroidery needle and size 11 seed beads.

38 Backstitch

Skill Level: Easy

Description: This is a basic line stitch. Insert the needle one stitch to the right and come back up two stitches to the left.

Beads: Example B: Add a size 11 bead to every other stitch. In example C, a size 11 bead is used in every stitch.

Here's How: Come up one space left of beginning, string one bead, insert needle at beginning and come up two spaces left of beginning. Repeat across to left.

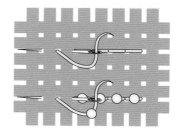

39 Half Cross

Skill Level: Easy

Description: This is one of the most common stitches for adding beads to embroidery. It is simply a diagonal stitch over one intersection of canvas threads.

Beads: In example B, a bead is used in every other stitch. This is a good method for using larger beads than will fit in every stitch.

In example C, a bead is used in every stitch. This pattern is dependent on the beads being the same size or smaller than the space between the holes in the canvas.

Here's How: Come up through canvas, string one bead, pass needle down through space diagonally up and to right, and come up one space down. Repeat across to right.

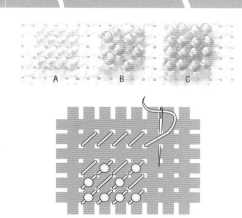

40 Cross

Skill Level: Easy

Description: This stitch is easy and quick to work and fills the square space with color. It is made of one diagonal stitch in one direction, then another diagonal stitch worked over the first, in the opposite direction.

Beads: Example B shows a bead added in between cross stitches. Add the beads with half cross stitches worked in the direction of the first part of the completed cross stitches.

Example C shows beads added to the second stitch in every other cross stitch.

Example D shows beads added to the second stitch in every cross stitch.

Here's How: Come up through canvas, pass needle down through space diagonally up and to right and come up one space down. Repeat across

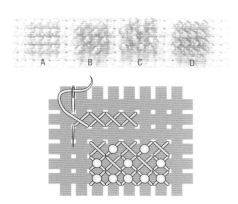

to right. Working to the left, string one bead, pass needle down through space diagonally up and to left and come up one space down. Repeat across, adding a bead to every stitch or every other stitch.

41 Cross Variation

Skill Level: Easy

Description: This is the same stitch as #40 Cross, except that it is worked over two canvas intersections, rather than one. It opens up more possibilities for bead treatments.

Beads: Example B uses two beads in the first half of the stitch, then the second half of the stitch goes between the two beads, holding them in place.

Example C uses two beads in each half of the stitch. When pulling the second stitch through, make sure that the beads lay on either side of the previous stitch.

Here's How: Come up through canvas, string two beads, pass down through second space diagonally up and to right, and come up two spaces down. Repeat across to right. Working to the left, string two beads, pass needle down through second space diagonally up and to left, and come up two spaces down, separating each pair of beads as you pull the thread through. Repeat across.

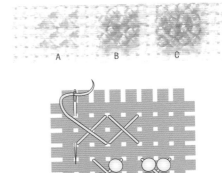

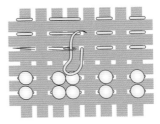

42 Darning

Also known as basting.

Skill Level: Easy

Description: Simply pass in and out of the fabric in a straight line. Changing the number of canvas intersections skipped can create many designs.

Beads: Add the same number of beads for each stitch as the number of canvas intersections covered.

Here's How: Come up through canvas, string enough beads to fill stitch, pass horizontally over one or more canvas intersections, go down and then come up one space away.

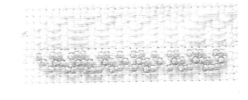

43 Arrowhead

Also known as double-sided Italian.

Skill Level: Intermediate

Description: This simple zigzag stitch can be worked as a line or as a dense surface pattern.

Beads: The beads transition from one bead in every other stitch to one bead in every stitch to three beads in each stitch.

Here's How: Come up through canvas, string one or two beads. Go down two spaces diagonally up and to right and come up two spaces diagonally down and to the right. *String one or two beads, enter and exit canvas in the same spaces again. String one or two beads, go down two spaces diagonally up and to right, come up two spaces diagonally down and to right. Repeat from asterisk.

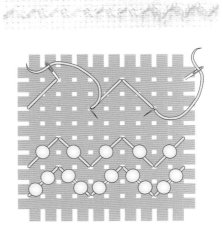

44 Herringbone

Also known as open herringbone.

Skill Level: Easy

Description: This basic crisscross stitch is the basis for many variations, one of which is shown next.

Beads: There are many ways to add beads to this stitch, from adding just one bead and catching it in the cross created by the next stitch, to adding enough beads to fill all the thread in the stitch. When using just a few beads in the stitch, it helps to go back and tack down where the threads cross to help hold the beads in place.

Here's How: Come up through canvas, string one bead, go down four spaces diagonally up and to right, and come up two spaces to left. String one bead, go down four spaces diagonally down and to right, and come up two spaces to left. Repeat, stringing one to four beads and positioning them as you pull the thread through. Add half-stitch at each end, if desired.

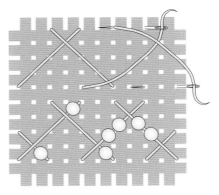

45 Threaded Herringbone

Skill Level: Intermediate

Description: After working herringbone stitch, weave in and out of the finished stitch. This is often done with a contrasting thread color.

Beads: Add beads to the threaded part of the stitch with up to three added to each pass of the thread. Another possibility is to work the whole piece in beads, making the whole stitch larger to accommodate all the beads.

Here's How: Stitch a row of #44 Herringbone. Come up one to two spaces above bottom of left-most stitch. *String one to three beads and slide needle under center section of first diagonal thread from bottom to top. String one to three beads and slide needle under center of next diagonal thread from top to bottom. Repeat from asterisk.

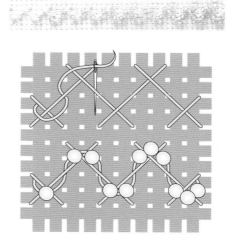

46 Chevron

Also known as open chevron.

Skill Level: Intermediate

Description: Consisting of backstitches and diagonal stitches, this stitch can be large or small, and open or tightly spaced.

Beads: Two beads fit perfectly on the backstitches along the top and bottom of this stitch. This stitch also works nicely completely filled with beads.

Here's How: Come up through canvas, *go down four spaces up and three spaces to right, and come up one space left. String two beads, go down two spaces right and come up one space left, exiting below the beaded stitch. Go down four spaces down and three spaces right, exiting one space left. String two beads, go down two spaces right and come up space left, exiting above beaded stitch. Repeat from asterisk.

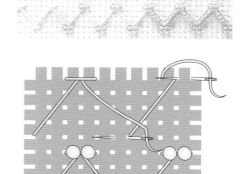

47 Blanket

Also known as spaced buttonhole stitch.

Skill Level: Intermediate

Description: Make a straight stitch, catching the loop of the thread in the stitch as the thread is pulled in place. On counted thread, it is easy to make this stitch uniform, and the options include long or short and open or dense.

Beads: Determine where the bead or beads end up when pulling the thread in place for this stitch. If stringing the bead and just pulling the stitch into place, the bead will end up at the top of the vertical part of the stitch. If sliding the bead to where the thread is coming out of the fabric, the bead will end up on the horizontal part of the stitch. Another option is to fill the stitch with beads, being careful to hold the number of beads in each section of the stitch, so when pulling the thread in place, the beads are in the correct position.

Here's How: Come up through canvas, string one or more beads. Holding the thread down and to the right, enter canvas diagonally up three spaces and come up three spaces down. The thread is caught in the stitch as you pull through, creating a backwards "L". Position the bead(s) on either side of the exiting thread as you pull through. Repeat across.

48 Cretan

Also known as long-armed feather, Persian, or quill.

Skill Level: Intermediate

Description: The technique of making this stitch is similar to Blanket stitch, though the direction to form the stitches is alternated. The stitch can be open or closed, creating a variety of effects.

Beads: This is a great stitch for adding beads since the looks vary so much; place beads in the vertical ends of the stitch, the middle, or fill the stitches with beads.

Here's How: Come up through canvas, string one or more beads. Holding the thread down and to the right, enter canvas up six spaces and two spaces to right, and then come up two spaces down. The thread is caught in the stitch as you pull through. *String one or more beads. Holding thread up and to right, enter canvas down four spaces and two spaces to right, and then come up two spaces up. String one or more beads. Holding thread down and to right, enter canvas up four spaces and two spaces to right, and then come up two spaces down. Repeat from asterisk, positioning bead(s) on either side of the exiting thread as you pull through.

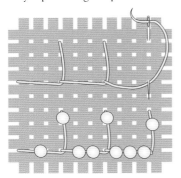

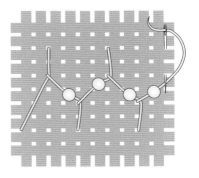

Pulled Thread, Drawn Work and Insertion Stitches

These stitches all depend on the manipulation of the base fabric in some way, from pulling the stitches tightly, to removing threads from the fabric, to embroidering a bridge between fabrics. All of these stitches have an interesting effect when worked with beads because the width of the bead determines the size of the finished stitch. In pulled thread stitches, for example, you can pull the threads very tightly without a bead in the stitch, but if you string a bead into the stitch you can only pull the thread to the width of the bead. In insertion stitches, this can be an advantage because if you fill the space of the stitch between the two fabrics with beads, you will ensure an even-length space all along the piece. Adding beads to these stitches adds texture and regularity to the stitches. All of the samples were made using size 8 pearl cotton and size 11 beads. The drawn thread samples were stitched on 22-count Hardanger cloth and the other two techniques were stitched on 25-count Dublin linen.

Pulled Thread

49 Coil Filling

Also known as pulled satin stitch, whipped satin stitch or whipstitch.

Skill Level: Easy

Description: This stitch consists of rows of three tightly-pulled satin stitches spaced between every four threads and offset from row to row. The three finished stitches should lay side by side, not overlapping each other.

Beads: Only one bead will fit in each group of three stitches. In an all-over surface design, use the beads for an added pattern in the design.

Here's How: Come up through fabric, *go down two spaces up, and then come up two spaces down. String one bead. Enter two spaces up, and come up two spaces down. Enter two spaces up and come up two spaces down and four right. Repeat from

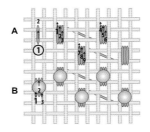

asterisk, pulling tightly so fabric is pulled in at each stitch. Stagger each row between previous stitches.

50 Faggot

Also known as single faggot.

Skill Level: Intermediate

Description: This diagonally-worked stitch, usually worked over four threads, stair steps across the fabric, making tightly pulled horizontal and vertical stitches. The back side of this stitch is also used in needlework and is called reversed faggot.

Beads: Place beads in either just the horizontal threads or vertical threads, or both.

Here's How: Come up through fabric. *String one bead. Enter fabric four spaces left, and come up four spaces diagonally down and right. String one bead. Enter fabric four spaces up, and come up four spaces diagonally down and right. Repeat from asterisk, pulling tightly so fabric is pulled in at each stitch. When turning on last stitch, come up four spaces diagonally down and left, rather than right. Turn fabric and repeat stitch pattern.

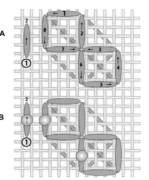

51 Diagonal Chained Border

Skill Level: Intermediate

Description: This is actually two rows of reverse faggot stitch turning direction every four repeats of the stitch, creating a zigzag border pattern.

Beads: Add beads to the center between stitches, or to all the stitches.

Here's How: Come up through fabric. *String one bead. Enter fabric diagonally up four spaces to right, and come up four spaces down. String one bead. Enter fabric diagonally up four spaces to right, and come up four spaces left. Repeat from asterisk, pulling tightly so fabric is pulled in at each stitch. To turn corner, omit bead from last stitch, rotate fabric upside-down and repeat second stitch in pattern, crossing over stitch just completed, and continue in pattern.

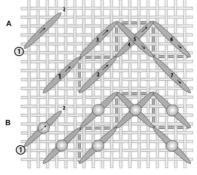

52 Four-Sided

Skill Level: Intermediate

Description: Work this basic stitch either in rows diagonally, as a filler or in a single line. The stitch is made over four threads, creating a tightly-pulled box shape.

Beads: Create different looks by using beads in just the vertical or horizontal stitches or create a dense beading effect using beads in all the stitches.

Here's How: Come up and *string one bead. Enter fabric four spaces up, and come up diagonally down four spaces to left. String one bead. Enter fabric four spaces right, and come up diagonally up four spaces to left. String one bead. Enter fabric four spaces to right, come up diagonally down four spaces to left. Repeat from asterisk, pulling at each

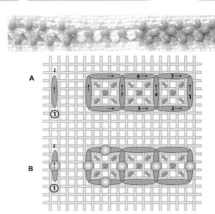

stitch. Leave some stitches without beads to create different designs, if desired.

Drawn Thread

53 Hem

Skill Level: Easy

Description: Work stitch at base of a drawn section with three or more threads removed. The stitch passes around a group of threads and then down through fabric before the next group of threads to be bundled. Work left to right, usually on the wrong side of fabric so diagonal stitches are on the wrong side and vertical stitches are on the right side. Notice here, however, that both the right (wrong side) and left (right side) sides of the top row are decorative and used for embroidery.

Beads: This sample is stitched over four threads for the bundles and the vertical stitches. Add one bead to horizontal stitches and one or two beads to vertical stitches. Since this stitch is worked from the wrong side of the fabric, help the beads slide into the correct position as you stitch.

Here's How: Pull out four horizontal threads. Working from back of fabric, bring needle up four spaces below drawn thread section on left side. *Pass needle from right to left under next

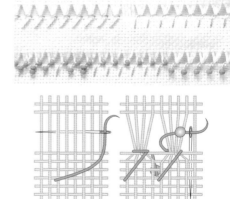

four threads to right in drawn section. Pull tightly. String one bead. Pass needle through space on right side of the four threads created by last stitch, behind fabric, and come up four spaces down, positioning bead on front side of fabric (which is facing away from you). Do not pull this part of stitch tight. Repeat from asterisk.

54 Ladder Hem

Skill Level: Intermediate

Description: This is hem stitch worked over both sides of a drawn section, bundling the same groups of threads on each side, creating a vertical bar of threads in the drawn section. Usually one or two more threads are drawn out for this stitch than for basic hem stitch.

Beads: This stitch has the same options for beads as hem stitch, but double the amount of beads.

Here's How: Pull out four to six horizontal threads. Work #53 Hem stitch along one edge of drawn section. Rotate fabric and work same stitch again, bundling the same threads as on first side.

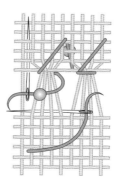

55 Zigzag Hem

Also known as serpentine hem or trellis hem.

Skill Level: Intermediate

Description: The same as #54 Ladder Hem stitch, except that the bundled threads are offset by half from one side to the other. You must have an even number of threads in each bundle, so you can split them on the other side of the drawn section.

Beads: This stitch has the same possible bead combinations as ladder hem stitch.

Here's How: Pull out four to six horizontal threads. Work #53 Hem stitch along one edge of drawn section. Rotate fabric and work same stitch again, bundling two threads from one stitch and two from the next stitch along first side.

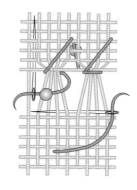

56 Italian Hem Variation

Skill Level: Intermediate

Description: This is pulled thread's four-sided stitch worked between two bars of drawn thread with a four-thread section between. For traditional Italian hem stitch, the other sides of the drawn sections would be stitched in hem stitch.

Beads: Because the threads here are not pulled as tightly as those in #52 Four-Sided stitch, more beads will fit in the stitches. For the horizontal stitches that wrap the bundles of threads, notice that the bundle isn't as tight when adding two beads to the stitch instead of just one.

Here's How: Pull out four horizontal threads, skip down four threads and pull out four more horizontal threads. Working along the center four threads, bring needle up to left of first four lower drawn threads. *Pass needle behind fabric, entering right of lower four drawn threads, and exiting diagonally up behind four threads of center

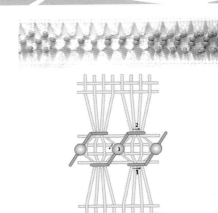

section and out to left of first four upper drawn threads. Pull tight. Pass from right to left behind first four upper drawn threads. Pull tight. String one bead. Pass from right to left behind next four lower drawn threads. Repeat from asterisk.

57 Interlaced Hem

Skill Level: Intermediate

Description: This is a ladder hem stitch that is twisted from bar to bar with a horizontal thread passing around the vertical bars, and pulled tightly to twist them. Also work over a wide drawn section so you can make several passes, for a lattice effect.

Beads: Make one pass of thread, twisting the vertical bars with size 8 and size 11 beads strung between the twisted bars.

Here's How: Pull out six horizontal threads and work #54 Ladder Hem along edges of drawn section. Working right to left in every two-thread bundle in drawn section, string one bead, pass needle from left to right behind left bundle and in front of right bundle. Flip needle from right to left, so two bundles switch positions in middle. Pull through. Repeat for each bundle pair.

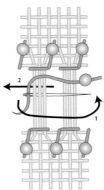

58 Cross

Skill Level: Intermediate

Description: Simple cross stitches are worked across the opening; insert the needle from back to front for each stitch and work across the row in one diagonal direction, and back the other way in the other diagonal direction.

Beads: Add beads to this stitch sparingly or completely, creating different effects.

Here's How: Fold over raw edges and baste two fabrics to be joined to a waste fabric, leaving ¼" between. Do not stitch through waste fabric. Bring needle out at left edge of top piece. *String three beads and take a stitch in the lower piece from back to front, about ¼" away. String three beads, take a stitch in the top piece from back to front, about

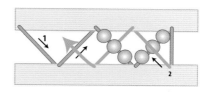

¼" away. Repeat from asterisk to end of fabrics. Take a stitch in the opposite fabric at the end of the row and work back across both fabrics with or without beads. Remove basting.

59 Zigzag

Skill Level: Easy

Description: This row of zigzagging diagonal stitches creates a quick bridge between fabric edges.

Beads: Filling this stitch with beads makes it easier to stitch, since the beads determine the spacing between the fabric edges.

Here's How: Fold over raw edges and baste two fabrics to be joined to a waste fabric, leaving ¼" between. Do not stitch through waste fabric. Bring needle out at left edge of upper piece. *String three beads and take a stitch in the lower piece from back to front, about ¼" away. String three beads and take a stitch in the top piece from back to front, about ¼" away. Repeat from asterisk to end of fabrics. Remove basting.

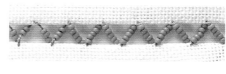

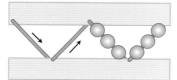

60 Threaded Zigzag

Skill Level: Intermediate

Description: This stitch is created by working a row of zigzag stitch, then weaving a second thread over and under the finished stitching.

Beads: Filling all the stitches with beads creates an interesting texture and pattern.

Here's How: Work #59 Zigzag on prepared fabrics. Bring needle out to left of completed stitching in upper fabric. String three beads, pass from top to bottom behind first stitch, string three beads and pass from bottom to top behind next stitch. Repeat across.

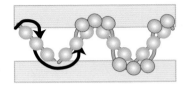

61 Half Cretan Insertion

Skill Level: Easy

Description: In this easy stitch, the thread on one edge of the fabric is caught in the thread coming out of the back of the stitch, but the stitch on the other edge is not. This creates a looped cross along one edge.

Beads: Add one or more beads to any part of this stitch, however, the beads may migrate if the stitch is long or if the finished piece will have any movement.

Here's How: Fold over raw edges and baste two fabrics to be joined to a waste fabric, leaving ¼" between. Do not stitch through waste fabric. Come up at left edge of bottom piece. *String one bead and take small stitch in top piece from front to back about ¼" away, with needle coming out on the left side of stitch. Take a small stitch on the bottom piece from back to front about ¼" away, with needle coming out on right side of stitch. Repeat from asterisk.

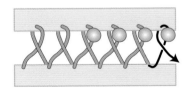

62 Open Cretan Insertion

Also known as faggot and herringbone insertion.

Skill Level: Intermediate

Description: Each side of the stitch comes out from behind the previous stitch, creating a twist at both ends of each stitch.

Beads: Added beads in this stitch stay in place except when there are a lot of beads in one section and none in the other.

Here's How: Fold over raw edges and baste two fabrics to be joined to a waste fabric, leaving ¼" between. Do not stitch through waste fabric. Come out at left edge of bottom piece. *Take a small stitch in top piece from front to back about ¼" away, with the needle coming out on the left side of stitch. String one bead and take small stitch in bottom piece from front to back about ¼" away, with needle coming out on left side of stitch. Repeat from asterisk.

63 Knotted Insertion

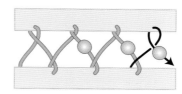

Also known as knotted herringbone insertion.

Skill Level: Advanced

Description: This is the #59 Zigzag stitch with knots added at the edge of the fabric.

Beads: Because of the knots, all of the beads will stay in place in any part of this stitch.

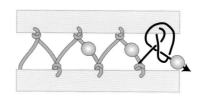

Here's How: Fold over raw edges and baste two fabrics to be joined to a waste fabric, leaving ¼" space between. Do not stitch through waste fabric. Come out at left edge of bottom piece. *Take a small stitch in top piece from front to back about ¼" away, with the needle coming out on the left side of stitch. Loop thread around to the right and pass needle under previous stitch and through loop, as shown, pulling to form knot close to fabric. String one bead and repeat the step on the bottom piece. Repeat from asterisk.

64 Grouped Blanket Insertion

Also known as buttonhole insertion.

Skill Level: Intermediate

Description: Three closely spaced blanket stitches on alternating edges of fabric create this stitch.

Beads: Adding beads to the thread between the fabric edges can be used to measure how far apart you want your fabric edges to be. You can also adjust the spacing of the groups of stitches based on the size beads you use and how many you add to the vertical parts of the stitches.

Here's How: Fold over raw edges and baste two fabrics to be joined to a waste fabric, leaving ¼" space between. Do not stitch through waste fabric. Come out at left edge of top piece, *loop thread down to right. Enter top fabric ⅛" diagonally up and to right, exiting at back of fabric with needle coming out from behind fabric so you catch the looped thread in stitch as you pull through. Repeat from asterisk twice more. String two to three beads and then stitch the same three stitches on the bottom fabric, reversing direction. Alternate the three blanket stitches on the upper and lower fabrics, separated by beads.

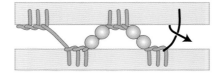

Hardanger

Hardanger is a form of Norwegian counted thread embroidery that combines primarily satin stitch, drawn threads and cutwork to create geometric, embroidered openwork fabric. Traditionally worked in white on white, today Hardanger is also worked in colored fabric and thread. Adding beads to Hardanger is not traditional, and because some of the stitches are structural to prepare the fabric for cutwork, you need to be selective in the placement of beads. Beads, however, can add a new dimension to this beautiful traditional technique. In the samples in this section, the Kloster blocks and motifs were worked in size 5 pearl cotton with size 8 bead embellishments and size 26 tapestry needle. The decorative stitching inside the cutwork was stitched using size 8 pearl cotton with size 11 beads and a size 28 tapestry needle. All the samples were worked on 22-count Hardanger cloth.

65 Kloster Blocks

Also known as satin stitch blocks.

Skill Level: Easy

Description: This is the basic cornerstone of all Hardanger embroidery. Projects incorporate these satin stitch blocks in a variety of arrangements. The satin stitches are usually worked in groups of five stitches over four threads using a thicker thread than the rest of the project, and are used as a design element as well as a basis for cutwork.

Beads: It's possible to replace the Kloster block stitches with rows of small beads, but I don't recommend adding beads to borders of cutwork sections because the beads might travel around to the back of the fabric after cutting. This example shows size 8 beads added between blocks, giving the embroidered section a more solid look.

Here's How: Come up, *enter fabric four spaces down, and come up four spaces up and one right. Repeat four more times, exiting four spaces right on last stitch. Work five of the same stitches horizontally and down, exiting last stitch four spaces right. Repeat five vertical stitches to the right, then five horizontal stitches down. Repeat

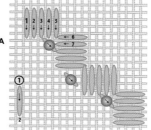

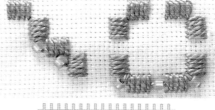

from asterisk. To add beads, come up at end of third stitch in first five-stitch cluster, string one bead and pass down in end of third stitch in next five-stitch cluster. Come up one space diagonally down and right of end of last stitch in current cluster, string one bead and then enter fabric two spaces diagonally down and right. Repeat for each cluster intersection.

66 Kloster Square

Also known as floral motif.

Skill Level: Easy

Description: This arrangement of Kloster blocks creates a square. Cut the center threads of the square for an openwork effect, or leave it as is.

Beads: Add the beads to the arrangement either after each block is completed or after the square is completed. If adding beads after the square is completed, pass the thread under the back side of the completed blocks to get to each corner.

Here's How: Stitch four five-stitch clusters so the end of each cluster shares the space of the last stitch in previous cluster, creating a square in the middle. To add beads as in B, come up at space where two clusters meet, string one bead and enter fabric two diagonal spaces away. Repeat in each corner.

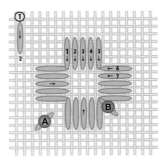

67 Small Star Motif

Skill Level: Easy

Description: This simple decorative star is made of stepped satin stitch bars.

Beads: The addition of the beads can greatly change the appearance of the pattern. In example A, the beads were added after pattern was completed. In example B, the beads were added as the motif was stitched, strung on for the four center-most stitches.

Here's How: Come up, enter fabric four spaces down, and come up five spaces up and one right. Repeat three more times, exiting four spaces to the right on last stitch. *Enter fabric four spaces left and exit three spaces right and one down. Repeat three more times, exiting five spaces right and one down on the last stitch. Enter fabric four spaces left and exit five spaces right and one down. Repeat two more times, exiting four spaces diagonally down and to left on last stitch. Rotate fabric and repeat from asterisk. To add beads

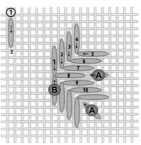

as in A, come up three stitches away diagonally from outermost intersecting stitches, string one bead and enter one stitch away from outermost intersecting stitches. Repeat at base of "V" created on shorter sides of design and around motif.

68 Large Star Motif

Also known as snowflake motif.

Skill Level: Intermediate

Description: Each leg of this larger star, or snowflake, begins by increasing the stitch length by one thread space with each stitch, then tapers to a point by decreasing on the opposite side.

Beads: Add the beads to the pattern stitches as the star is made. To work the beads into the design, start by stringing a bead for the first stitch and the last stitch of each section of the star shape.

Here's How: Come up, string one bead, enter fabric two spaces up, and exit two spaces down and one right. Enter fabric three spaces up, exiting three spaces down and one right. Repeat, making each stitch one space longer until there are six. On sixth stitch, exit fabric one space up from other stitches. Continue to the right, keeping tops of stitches even with sixth stitch and decreasing length of each stitch by one until there are 11 stitches,

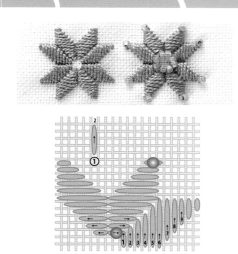

stringing one bead before completing last stitch. Repeat pattern in mirror image, rotate fabric and stitch three more pairs of diamond clusters.

69 Diamond Motif

Skill Level: Intermediate

Description: This simple convergence of triangle shapes creates a pinwheel diamond that can be used in a group arrangement or alone.

Beads: Add the beads to the pattern stitches as the diamond is made. To work the beads into the design, work the stitch, adding one bead to the stitches that cover two threads of the fabric, then also add one to the center.

Here's How: Come up, enter fabric eight spaces up, and exit eight spaces down and one right. Enter seven spaces up, exiting seven spaces down and one right. Continue vertical stitches to the right, making each one space shorter than the one before, stringing one bead before completing the seventh stitch. Make one more stitch over one thread. Come up one space below first stitch, rotate fabric and repeat eight-stitch triangle. Make two more

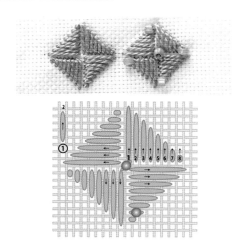

triangles. Come up at base of third triangle, string one bead and enter fabric two spaces diagonally up and right.

70 Triangle Border

Also known as satin fringe motif.

Skill Level: Easy

Description: This simple triangle creates an elegant edging when stitched in a row.

Beads: Add beads to the stitches as the triangle border is made. Add them to shortest stitch in each triangle, at the triangle points and in the corner.

Here's How: Come up, enter fabric two spaces up, and exit two spaces down and one left. Enter fabric three spaces up, exiting three spaces down and one left. Continue vertical stitches to the left, making each one space longer until you have five stitches. Then make four stitches, each one space shorter until there are nine total, bringing needle up two spaces to left after last stitch. String one bead, enter fabric two spaces diagonally up and right, and exit two spaces left. Rotate fabric and repeat nine stitches, counting last stitch in repeat as first stitch in next repeat.

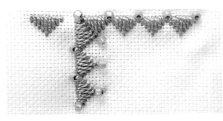

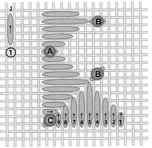

71 Tulip Variation

Skill Level: Intermediate

Description: This geometric flower is made of two satin stitches similar to sections of the large star motif (#68) with curls added to the ends.

Beads: Add beads in many ways to enhance this simple design. In this example, place one bead at tips of the petals and three at center for a stamen. Also try beads at the base of the flower.

Here's How: Come up, enter fabric two spaces up, and exit two spaces down and one right. Enter three spaces up and exit three spaces down and one right. Repeat, making each stitch one space longer until there are five. On fifth stitch, exit one space up from other stitches. Continue to the right, keeping tops of stitches even with fifth stitch and decreasing length of each stitch by one until there are nine. Make two stitches the same size as ninth stitch and two more stitches the same size, but stepping down one space. Come up two spaces diagonally down and left of base of last stitch,

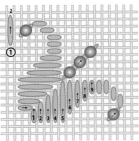

string one bead and enter at base of last stitch. Repeat in mirror image. Come up at top of fifth stitch, string three beads, and enter five spaces diagonally up and right.

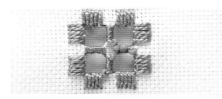

72 Wrapped Bar

Also known as overcast bars.

Skill Level: Intermediate

Description: After threads are cut for openwork, embellish remaining threads by wrapping them into a bundle to pull threads into a narrow bar.

Beads: Add beads at any time while making the bar. Here, the top bar has a bead in center. The next bar to the right has a bead at beginning, middle and end, with two wraps between each wrap. The last bar has a bead on first and last wrap. The beads tend to lean, so if you are particular about beads staying where you stitch them, don't add beads.

Here's How: Stitch two Kloster blocks at right angles, *skipping four vertical threads and stitching two more blocks at right angles. Repeat twice from asterisk. Cut and remove inner threads close to blocks. Anchor thread in back of block adjacent to base of four center threads. Come up in one opening of cut threads, pass around four threads, pulling tightly and keeping wrap close to base of threads. Repeat wrap, string one bead, repeat wrap, positioning bead to front. Repeat wraps, covering four threads and adding beads every three stitches.

73 Woven Bar

Skill Level: Intermediate

Description: Alternately stitch around two threads of the four threads in the cutwork, creating two satin stitched bars woven together.

Beads: Add beads to this stitch simply by stringing a bead and completing the stitch. The beads stay where stitched a little better than in #72 Wrapped Bar, but they still can travel.

Here's How: Stitch Kloster squares as in #72, and cut and remove threads. Anchor thread in back of Kloster block adjacent to base of four center threads. Pass over two threads and under two threads. Stitching in opposite direction, pass over last two threads and under first two threads, forming loops down to base of threads and keeping stitches even. Repeat to center of threads. String one bead, pass over and under two threads, string one bead, and pass over and under two threads in opposite direction. Repeat stitch without beads until threads are covered.

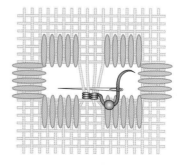

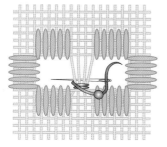

74 Woven Bar with Picot

Skill Level: Intermediate

Description: In this technique, work a woven bar halfway, make a picot stitch on each side, then complete the bar.

Beads: In this example, beads are added to the picot. One or three beads work well when added to the picot stitch, but notice how the bottom treatment with two beads doesn't stay flat.

Here's How: Work same as #73 to center of four threads, ending on left side. For beaded picots, string one bead, pass under left two threads from right to left, pass over, under and over, working thread as shown. Pull through. Pass over and under four threads and repeat on other side. Finish woven bar, covering threads.

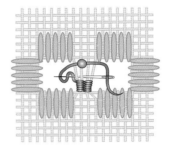

75 Dove's Eye Filling

Also known as dove's eye.

Skill Level: Intermediate

Description: This is a twisted stitch worked into each corner of the opening, creating a lacy diamond effect in the center of the cutwork section.

Beads: Example A shows one bead added to two of the stitches, and example B shows one bead added to every stitch. Example C shows one bead added to every stitch so that the beads are in the twisted section, not the center diamond shape.

Here's How: Example in Kloster square: Stitch Kloster square, and cut and remove center threads. Come up in center of one Kloster block, string one bead and enter adjacent center of block, passing under thread to form loop as you pull through. Position bead before or after crossing of stitches. Repeat in each block, passing over last thread and into back of first block to complete.

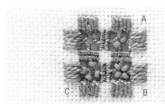

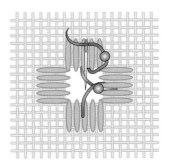

Freeform Embroidery

Freeform embroidery is a versatile technique with both structure and the opportunity for creativity. When adding beads to the stitches, you have many options, from just adding one bead to filling the stitches with beads so that the beads determine the size and placement of the stitches. Many stitches contain loops or overlap previous stitches which gives you the choice of adding a bead or beads to either the first or second part of the stitch. Most of the samples in this section show a progression of bead ideas, beginning with one bead added and progressing to most, or all, of the stitch filled with beads. The samples were all worked with size 11 beads, but some were stitched on thin cotton with two strands of embroidery floss, and others were stitched with size 8 pearl cotton on cotton gabardine.

76 Running

Skill Level: Easy

Description: The simplest of stitches, this pattern is made by passing in and out of the fabric at even intervals, making a straight or curved line.

Beads: This stitch is usually worked by passing in and out of the fabric several times before pulling the needle through. When adding beads, however, make only one stitch at a time.

Here's How: Come up, string one bead, enter fabric one bead's width away and exit a short distance away, usually the same width or shorter than the stitch. Repeat across.

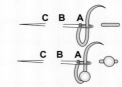

77 Backstitch

Skill Level: Easy

Description: This stitch is made by inserting the needle one stitch length behind the direction of stitching and coming out of the fabric two stitch lengths in front of the point where the needle entered the fabric. It creates a continual, sturdy line of stitching.

Beads: Accent this stitch with one bead or fill it with beads. When making a continuous line, the number of beads used in the stitch will determine the size of the backstitch.

Here's How: Come up, string one bead, enter fabric one bead's width to right and exit two bead's widths to left. Repeat across.

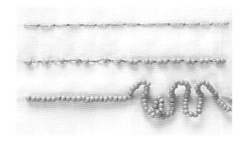

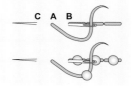

78 Threaded Backstitch

Also known as laced backstitch.

Skill Level: Easy

Description: Once a row of backstitch is complete, use a blunt-ended needle, such as a tapestry needle, to weave in and out of the finished backstitch.

Beads: This example shows the beads added to the stitches that were threaded through the backstitch (though another option is to put the beads in the backstitches).

Here's How: Come up, enter fabric ⅛" to right and exiting ¼" to left. Repeat across. Come up at beginning of stitch. Passing behind stitching and not piercing fabric, pass down behind first stitch, string one bead, pass up behind next stitch, string one bead and pass down behind next stitch. Repeat across.

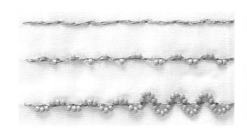

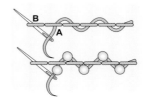

79 Double Threaded Backstitch

Also known as interlaced backstitch.

Skill Level: Easy

Description: After completing threaded backstitch, add one more line of threaded stitches, passing in and out of the backstitches in the opposite direction of the first row.

Beads: Notice that double threaded backstitch looks much different than threaded backstitch (#78). This stitch has more bead combination options to use in each stitch along the row.

Here's How: Stitch #78 Threaded Backstitch. Then, come up at beginning of stitch and pass up behind first stitch. String one bead, pass down behind next stitch, string one bead and pass up behind next stitch. Repeat across.

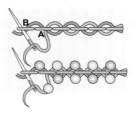

80 Split

Also known as Kensington outline.

Skill Level: Easy

Description: Make a small backstitch, piercing the thread of the previous stitch as the needle comes out of the fabric. This stitch works very well with two strands of embroidery floss, since the two threads part as the needle comes up through the stitch.

Beads: This stitch looks very different depending on whether the bead is in the first part of the stitch, as shown in the illustration, or if the bead is in the last part of the stitch, so the two strands of floss straddle it, as shown in the example (middle row on the right).

Here's How: Come up and string one bead, sliding it all the way down the thread. Lay thread flat in direction of stitch and take a small stitch toward bead, piercing the thread as you pull through. Repeat across.

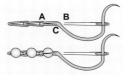

81 Stem

Also known as outline.

Skill Level: Easy

Description: Make this stitch, worked from left to right, by taking a short backstitch on the right side of the fabric, about half the width of the finished stitch. When this stitch is worked with the thread below the needle, it is called stem stitch. When it is worked with the thread above the needle, it is called outline stitch.

Beads: Whether one bead is added and pushed down to the base of this stitch, or allowed to slide to the end of the stitch, doesn't matter much in this stitch. Notice the rope effect when the stitches are filled with beads (bottom row on the right).

Here's How: Come up at A, string one bead, enter fabric at B and exit at C. Repeat.

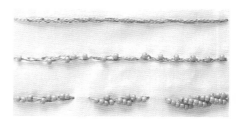

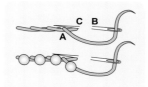

82 Straight

Also known as stroke.

Skill Level: Easy

Description: Make simple long or short stitches in any direction.

Beads: Add just one or two beads to this stitch, or fill the stitch with beads.

Here's How: Come up at A, string one or more beads, enter fabric at B and exit at C. Begin next stitch at C.

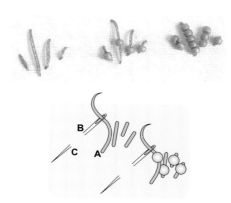

83 Seed

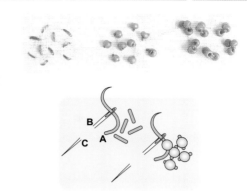

Also known as rice.

Skill Level: Easy

Description: This stitch is just small, even stitches stitched in random directions, all evenly spaced.

Beads: This stitch looks great with one or three beads in the stitch. The three-bead technique adds a raised texture to the stitch.

Here's How: Come up at A, string one bead, enter fabric at B and exit at C. Begin next stitch at C.

84 Satin

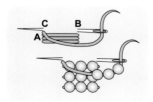

Skill Level: Easy

Description: This stitch is made of straight parallel side-by-side stitches that fill in a section of fabric with color.

Beads: When using beads in this stitch, the beads determine how long the stitch will be and how close the stitches are to each other.

Here's How: Come up at A, string enough beads to fill desired width of stitch, slide beads down to fabric. Enter fabric at end of last bead and exit near A, about one bead's width away. Repeat.

85 Padded Satin

Also known as raised satin.

Skill Level: Easy

Description: Stitch a layer of satin or chain stitches, then pass over them in a perpendicular direction to create a raised effect.

Beads: When working over a base of stitching, the beads raise up even more than the threads.

Here's How: Make straight stitches across design area in opposite direction planned for beaded stitches. To add beads, come up at one end of straight stitches and string enough beads to cover width of stitches. Enter fabric at end of last bead, covering straight stitches. Come up near beginning of beaded stitch. Repeat until straight stitches are covered.

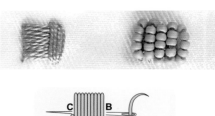

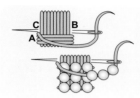

86 Cross

Also known as sampler.

Skill Level: Easy

Description: These simple X's are used in countless patterns, from cross stitch samplers to embroidered napkins. Complete each X individually, or make all the right slanting stitches for a row of stitches, then go back and make the left slanting stitches.

Beads: There is a surprising number of options for adding beads in this one little stitch. For instance, add the same number of beads to each half of the stitch or have one side of the stitch filled with beads while the other just has two on one side. To fill the X shape with beads, stitch four beads in the first stitch, making the stitch long enough so there is room for one more bead, then string five beads in the second half of the stitch so the beads fill the stitch, with the middle bead filling in the center space on the first half of the stitch.

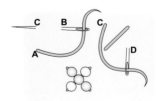

Here's How: Come up at A, string two beads, enter fabric at B and exit at C. String three beads and enter at D, straddling first two beads on either side of three beads as you pull stitch in place.

87 St. George's Cross

Also known as upright cross.

Skill Level: Easy

Description: This stitch looks like a plus sign and presents a whole different look than the #86 Cross stitch, even though it is the same stitch rotated 45 degrees.

Beads: The bead arrangements shown here can also be used for #86 Cross stitch and vice versa. The stitches on this example are a little smaller, so the stitch easily accommodates two beads in each half of the stitch, one in each leg, while the cross stitches are a little larger, so they can hold more beads.

Here's How: Come up at A, string two beads, enter fabric at B and exit at C. String two beads and enter at D, straddling first two beads on either side of two beads as you pull stitch in place.

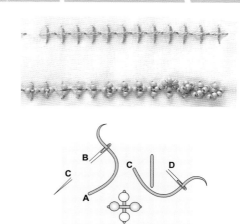

88 Herringbone

Skill Level: Easy

Description: Create these offset crossed lines by taking a backstitch along one line of the design, then taking another backstitch a little further away on the next line. The stitches can be worked close together or far apart.

Beads: Beads slid in the overlapping threads of this stitch tend to slide out of place, so it helps to stitch a row of backstitch over the intersections to make sure the beads will stay where you place them. This is actually a variation of the stitch called backstitched herringbone.

Here's How: Come up at A, string one bead, enter fabric at B and exit at C. String one bead, enter at D and exit at E. Repeat across.

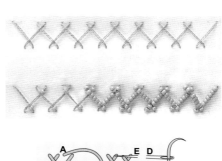

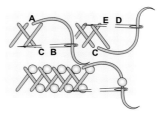

89 Threaded Herringbone

Skill Level: Easy

Description: Complete a row of herringbone stitch, then go back across the row and pass between the stitches with a new or contrasting length of thread to make threaded herringbone stitch.

Beads: This progression shows beads added to the first row of herringbone stitch, as well as beads added in the threading process.

Here's How: Stitch #88 Herringbone, adding two beads to each stitch and sliding each to one end of the stitch as you complete it. Come up at top of one end of stitch and pass down and under center of first stitch, being careful not to pierce fabric. Pass up and under center of next stitch. Repeat across, keeping beads at ends of stitch.

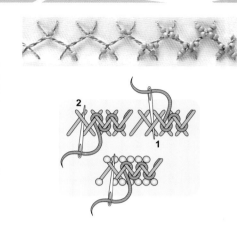

90 Chevron

Skill Level: Intermediate

Description: This stitch is made of zigzags bordered by small backstitches at the points.

Beads: This stitch looks very different with beads in the backstitches only. Filling the stitches with beads helps keep the stitches uniform, because you just have to count the same number of beads each time to make sure the stitch lengths are equal.

Here's How: Come up at A, enter fabric at B, exit at C, string two beads, enter at D and exit at E. Repeat pattern, alternating above and below about ¼" distance.

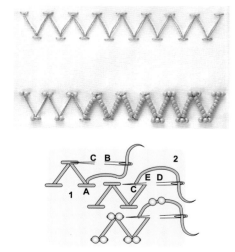

91 Arrowhead

Skill Level: Easy

Description: This stitch resembles #90 Chevron without the horizontal backstitches. It is an easy stitch that can be stitched large or small, open or dense.

Beads: Add beads to just one half of this stitch or the whole stitch. Each treatment presents a different look.

Here's How: Come up at A, string four beads, enter fabric at B and exit at C. Enter at B, exit at C, string four beads, enter at D and exit at E. Repeat across.

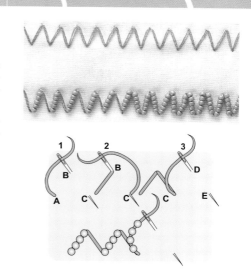

92 Chain

Skill Level: Easy

Description: Begin each new stitch in a loop created by the previous stitch.

Beads: There are many bead possibilities in this stitch, as shown in the example. One option is to place beads in either side of the loop. The number of beads used for the stitch greatly affects the finished appearance, as shown in the bottom lines of stitching.

Here's How: Come up at A, string one bead and slide it down thread, looping thread around as shown. Enter fabric at B and exit at C. Pull through, forming loop. Repeat.

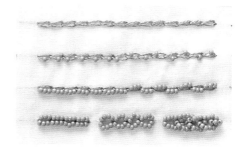

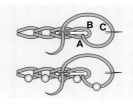

93 Lazy Daisy

Also known as detached chain.

Skill Level: Easy

Description: These little tacked-down loops are single chain stitches.

Beads: Place a bead or beads in the small tacking stitch, elongating it to accommodate the beads, or place beads in the loop of the stitch. This stitch has all the same possibilities as chain stitch.

Here's How: Come up at A, string one bead and slide it down thread, looping thread around as shown. Enter fabric at B and exit at C. Pull through, forming loop. Pass into fabric at D.

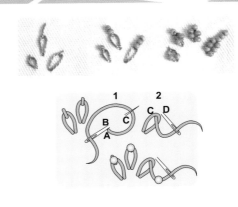

94 Open Chain

Skill Level: Intermediate

Description: This is the same as chain stitch except that instead of coming in and out of the fabric at the same place for the base of the loop, the stitches are spread apart. It's a little tricky, because you have to hold the forming loop open enough so you can take the next stitch creating the ladder effect.

Beads: In addition to the bead placements in chain stitch, the beads can also be placed in the center section of the stitch.

Here's How: Come up at A, string one bead and slide it down thread, looping thread around as shown. Enter fabric at B and exit at C. Pull through, forming loose loop. Enter fabric at top of loop for next stitch and finish pulling loop to size. Repeat.

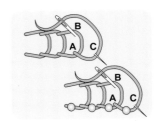

95 Whipped Chain

Skill Level: Easy

Description: This stitch is chain stitch with another thread passed around the stitch.

Beads: This example shows beads added to the thread passing around the chain stitch, though the beads could also be in the chain stitch.

Here's How: Make #92 Chain. Come up at end of last chain, string one bead and slide needle under chain from bottom to top, being careful not to pierce chain or base fabric. Repeat for each chain stitch.

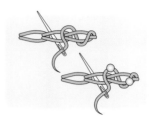

96 Backstitched Chain

Skill Level: Easy

Description: This is a row of chain stitches with backstitches worked over the completed stitch. Each backstitch passes over the junction of the chain stitches.

Beads: This example shows beads in the chain stitches and beads in the backstitches.

Here's How: Make #92 Chain. Come up at end of last chain, inside loop (A), string one bead, enter fabric at end of chain (B) and exit inside loop of next chain (C). Repeat.

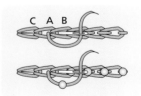

97 Wheat Ear

Skill Level: Intermediate

Description: This stitch is a combination of chain stitches and diagonal stitches.

Beads: Place beads in the straight stitches or only the chain stitches, or both.

Here's How: Come up at A, string one bead and slide it down thread. Enter fabric at B, exit at C, string one bead and slide it down thread. Enter at D, exit at E and slide needle under two stitches from top to bottom, being careful not to pierce fabric. Enter at F and exit at G. Repeat.

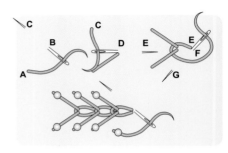

98 Pekinese

Skill Level: Easy

Description: This is a row of backstitches with loops laced in and out of the backstitches.

Beads: This is a wonderful stitch for adding beads, since there are so many options for placement, from the number of beads, to the top or bottom of the loops, to the backstitches themselves.

Here's How: Make a line of #77 Backstitch. Come up at end of stitches. Skip first stitch and slide needle up through next stitch, being careful not to pierce stitch or fabric. String one bead and slide needle down through skipped stitch. Repeat across.

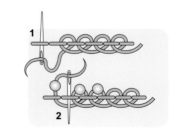

99 Double Pekinese

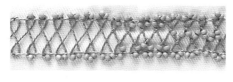

Skill Level: Intermediate

Description: Work two rows of backstitch, then lace between them to create a completely different look than plain #98 Pekinese stitch.

Beads: To hold the beads in place on the lacing steps of this stitch, go back and tack down the intersections of thread with vertical stitches.

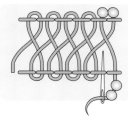

Here's How: Make two lines of #77 Backstitch spaced about ¼" away. Bring needle up at end of bottom line of stitches. Skip first stitch in upper line of stitches and slide needle up through next stitch, being careful not to pierce stitch or base fabric. String two beads and pass needle down through skipped stitch. Repeat across, alternating in bottom two stitches and then top two stitches.

100 Sheaf

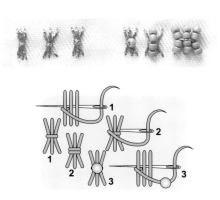

Skill Level: Intermediate

Description: This stitch is made of three vertical stitches with a horizontal stitch passing around them, cinching them together. The vertical stitches can be close together or spaced slightly apart.

Beads: Look how much the beads affect this stitch when they are used for the vertical stitches. To make this the same proportion as the non-beaded stitch, make the vertical stitches at least twice as long.

Here's How: Make three vertical stitches spaced slightly apart. Come up behind center of stitches, string one bead and pass back into fabric behind center of stitches, cinching vertical stitches together as you pull tightly.

101 Lock

Skill Level: Intermediate

Description: Stitch a row of evenly-spaced vertical stitches, then weave in and out of them twice, once along the top edge and once along the bottom edge, joining them together in a chain-like look.

Beads: To create the same look as the example, add beads to both the vertical and lacing stitches.

Here's How: Make row of vertical stitches with two beads in each stitch, spaced apart about half as much as their lengths. Come up just inside top of last stitch, slide one bead of first two stitches up to top end of stitches and pass needle under last stitch toward end of row, being careful not to pierce stitch or fabric. Pass under next stitch in opposite direction, exiting toward the top and catching beads in loop created as you pull through.

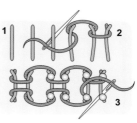

Pass needle under next stitch in opposite direction, exiting toward the bottom. Repeat across top and then repeat along bottom of vertical stitches.

102 Fishbone

Skill Level: Intermediate

Description: This center overlapping of diagonal stitches can be stitched close together for a satin stitch effect, or it can be stitched with space between the stitches.

Beads: To achieve the look of this example, fill all of the stitches with beads.

Here's How: Come up at A, string three beads, enter fabric at B, exit at C, string three beads, enter at D and exit at E. Repeat. To make first stitches smaller, begin with one bead in each stitch, then two and then three.

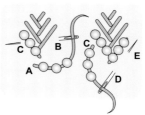

103 Fern

Skill Level: Intermediate

Description: This stitch is a V-shape with a vertical line passing through the center, resembling the stem and leaves of a fern plant.

Beads: Accentuate the "stem," "leaves" or both by choosing where in the stitch to place the beads.

Here's How: Come up at A, string two beads, enter fabric at B, exit at C, string two beads, enter at D, exit at E, string two beads, enter at F and exit at G. Repeat.

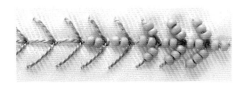

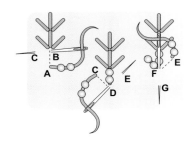

104 Leaf

Also known as fir.

Skill Level: Intermediate

Description: With its offset radiating diagonal lines of stitches, this stitch resembles a plant, especially if making the stitches smaller at one end to create the point of a leaf.

Beads: This example shows the stitch filled with beads.

Here's How: Come up at A, string enough beads to fill stitch, enter fabric at B, exit at C, string enough beads to fill stitch, enter at D and exit fabric at E.

105 Romanian

Skill Level: Intermediate

Description: This stitch is made of closely-stitched satin stitches tacked down at the center with a small diagonal stitch on each.

Beads: Place beads in the small diagonal stitch, on one or both sides of the satin stitch, or in all the parts of the stitch. Notice how you need to space the stitches farther apart when adding beads.

Here's How: Come up at A, enter fabric at B, exit at C, string one bead, enter at D and exit at E. Repeat two to three times with no beads, then stitch once with bead. Repeat.

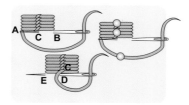

106 Blanket

Also known as buttonhole or open buttonhole.

Skill Level: Easy

Description: This easy and versatile stitch is made by taking a straight stitch from top to bottom along the side of an imaginary (usually ¼") box, and catching the thread in the stitch as you pull through.

Beads: There are many possibilities for this stitch when adding beads. You can just add one as you stitch and the bead will end up at the top of the stitch, or you can add one and slide it down to the fabric so it ends up caught in the horizontal part of the stitch. You can vary the number and types of beads you add to the stitch.

Here's How: Come up at A, string one or more beads, loop thread down and to right, enter fabric at B and exit at C, sliding beads into place as you pull stitch through.

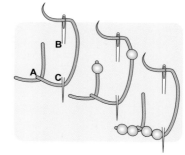

107 Buttonhole

Skill Level: Easy

Description: This is a very closely-stitched version of blanket stitch (#106).

Beads: The width of the beads prevents making a true buttonhole stitch unless the stitch is large enough to be in proportion to the beads. This example shows beads added to both parts of the stitch, but with the stitches spaced a little farther apart than normal.

Here's How: Come up at A, string one or more beads, loop thread down and to right, enter fabric at B and exit at C, sliding beads into place as you pull stitch through.

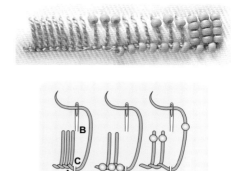

108 Closed Blanket

Skill Level: Intermediate

Description: In this variation of blanket stitch, each pair of vertical stitches begins at the same point to achieve a row of triangles.

Beads: Adding beads to the sides of this stitch creates a different look than when used in basic blanket stitch.

Here's How: Come up at A, loop thread down and to right, enter fabric at B, exit at C, string two beads and slide them down to fabric, loop thread down and to right, enter at D and exit at E. Repeat.

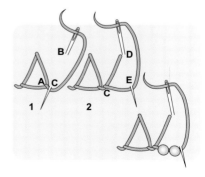

109 Cretan

Skill Level: Easy

Description: Alternating vertical stitches catch each previous loop in the stitch, creating a center ridge.

Beads: Add beads to the center or ends of this stitch. Because of the way the stitch locks in place, the beads in this stitch stay in place without the need for tacking intersections down.

Here's How: Come up at A, string three beads, loop thread down and to right, enter fabric at B, exit at C, string three beads, loop thread up and to right, enter at D and exit at E. Repeat.

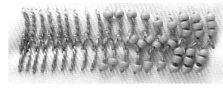

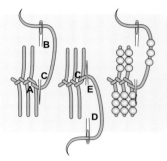

110 Open Cretan

Also known as long-armed feather.

Skill Level: Easy

Description: This is the same stitch as #109 Cretan, just stitched with more space between stitches.

Beads: As with #109 Cretan, the beads will stay in any section of this stitch without worry of them sliding out of place.

Here's How: Come up at A, string two beads and slide one down to fabric, loop thread down and to right, enter fabric at B, exit at C, string two beads and slide one down to fabric, loop thread up and to right, enter at D and exit at E. Repeat.

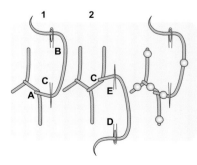

111 Fly

Skill Level: Easy

Description: These loops of thread, caught with a small stitch anchored somewhat below the stitch to create a V-shape, can be worked detached or in a line.

Beads: The placement of beads in this stitch can accent the small tacking stitch, fly part of the stitch, or both.

Here's How: Come up at A, enter fabric at B, exit at C, string one bead and enter at D.

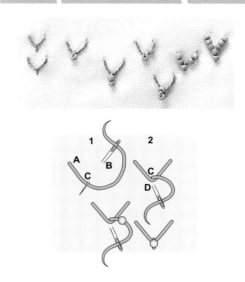

112 Feather

Skill Level: Easy

Description: Make a loop, then begin the next stitch by catching the loop at the beginning of the stitch. Make each successive stitch on alternate sides of the one before it for a branching effect.

Beads: Adding one or two beads to this stitch makes it look like a branch with little flower buds at the end.

Here's How: Come up at A, string one bead and slide it down to fabric, enter fabric at B, exit at C, string one bead, enter at D, exit at E, string one bead, enter at F and exit at G. Repeat.

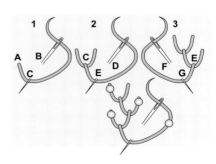

113 Double Feather

Also known as triple feather.

Skill Level: Intermediate

Description: This stitch is the same as feather stitch, but make several stitches on the same side of each previous stitch and then switch and make several stitches on the other side of each previous stitch. Sometimes people differentiate between double and triple feather by the number of stitches before a turn.

Beads: Beads added to this stitch resemble berries or flower buds on branches.

Here's How: Come up at A, string two beads, enter fabric at B, exit at C, string two beads, enter at D and exit at E. Repeat in same direction and then change direction for several stitches, switching direction for the same number of stitches each time.

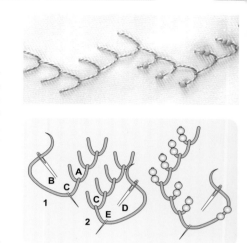

114 Van Dyke

Skill Level: Intermediate

Description: This column of horizontal stitches, looped around the previous stitch in the center, creates a chained rib in the center of radiating lines of stitches. The stitches can be long or short in different variations of the stitch.

Beads: It's difficult to add beads to the looped section of this stitch, and filling each stitch with beads (as shown in the example) can make the center secton pull. To avoid these problems, use beads in every other sttich or only use one or two beads in each stitch.

Here's How: Come up at A, string two beads and slide them down to fabric, enter fabric at B, exit at C, string two beads, enter at D, exit at E, *string two beads and slide them down to fabric. Slide behind stitches at F, being careful not to pierce stitches or fabric. String two beads, enter fabric below stitch at right end, exiting below stitch on left end (below D and E). Repeat from asterisk.

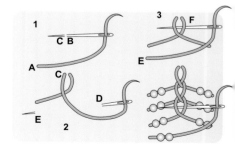

115 French Knot

Skill Level: Intermediate

Description: These small knots on the surface of the fabric are used in all sorts of embroidery as accents and details, and often have the same effect as beads.

Beads: To add a bead or beads to this stitch, string the beads, then wind the thread around the needle and insert the needle into the fabric. The final placement of the bead is dependent on whether you slide the bead down to the fabric before wrapping the needle or wrap the needle with the bead on the thread to pull through.

Here's How: Come up, string one bead, wrap thread around needle as shown and insert needle in fabric close to thread, holding knot as you pull through.

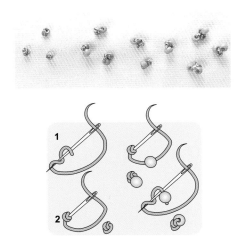

116 Turkey Work

Skill Level: Intermediate

Description: This stitch is made of a row of backstitches with loops held on the front of the fabric between stitches. Cutting the loops creates a furry look to the stitching.

Beads: Add beads to the backstitches or the loops, but don't cut the loops if adding beads to them!

Here's How: Come up at A, string two beads, enter fabric at B, exit at C with needle coming out below stitch, enter at D and exit at E with needle coming out above stitch, pulling just enough to leave a loop. Repeat, making all the loops the same size.

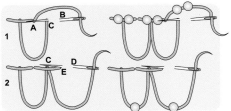

117 Cloud Filling

Skill Level: Intermediate

Description: Make this surface pattern by first stitching rows of small vertical stitches, with each row offset from the previous one and the stitches and rows an equal distance apart (¼" in this example). Then weave in and out of the stitches, alternating rows and repeating between each row, stitching in a mirror image from the row before, filling the surface with wavy lines.

Beads: Add beads to any part of this stitch. Notice that the section filled with beads is distorted. To keep the look of the original pattern when filling with beads, enlarge the spacing between the small vertical stitches.

Here's How: Make rows of small vertical stitches, offsetting each row by half, so every alternate row lines up. Come up on outside edge of last stitch in first row and slide needle through stitch, being careful not to pierce stitch or fabric. String one bead, slide under next stitch on next row, string one bead and slide under next stitch on first row. Repeat across two rows. Repeat process between the second and third row, and so on.

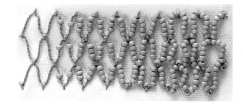

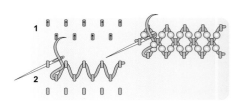

118 Coral

Also known as beaded.

Skill Level: Intermediate

Description: This is a row of thread tacked down with equally spaced knots as it is stitched.

Beads: Add beads in the knots, on the thread between the knots, or both.

Here's How: Come up, string two beads and slide them down to fabric. Holding thread down in stitch direction, take a small vertical stitch in fabric, just beyond beads, looping the remaining thread behind the needle as you pull through. Repeat.

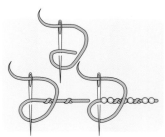

119 Couching

Skill Level: Easy

Description: Lay one thread in place and use another thread to take small stitches, tacking the first thread in place. Usually the first thread is thicker and often decorative, while the tacking thread is thin and inconspicuous.

Beads: This is a common stitch used for bead embroidery. Make a small tacking stitch between each bead or every few beads to hold them in place, or, as the last section of the example shows, add a bead to the tacking stitch, though it is not a common treatment.

Here's How: Come up, string enough beads to fill stitch, enter fabric, come up after several beads and take a small stitch over the thread, anchoring it in place. Repeat small stitch every two to four beads.

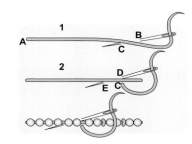

120 Couched Filling

Also known as trellis couching and trellis filling.

Skill Level: Intermediate

Description: In this surface stitch, lines of long diagonal stitches crisscross across the area to be stitched. Go back and take a small stitch over all the intersections of threads, tacking them in place. Another option is to make two small tacking stitches at right angles, creating a small #87 St. George's cross stitch.

Beads: This example shows beads added to the tacking stitches including some St. George's cross stitches. Another option is to fill the diagonal stitches with beads instead of the tacking stitches.

Here's How: Stitch diagonal lines over a grid, spaced ¼" to ⅜" apart. Come up at one intersection of two threads, string one bead, pass down into fabric on opposite side of thread intersection. Repeat for each thread intersection.

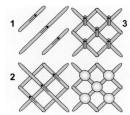

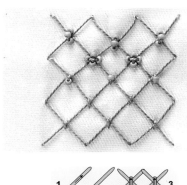

Crazy Quilt Stitches

Crazy quilt stitches can be considered a continuation of freeform embroidery, just with more embellishment. Most of them are variations of basic freeform embroidery, and for some that are already in the freeform section, I've shown here with more elaborate bead embellishment. Crazy quilting is one of the few embroidery stitches that has often been used with beads; the more elaborate the stitches, the better in crazy quilt embroidery. These samples were made using size 8 pearl cotton, size 11 beads and gabardine cotton.

121 Overlapping Blanket

Skill Level: Easy

Description: This is simply a row #106 Blanket with a second row overlapping the first row, just a little bit in offset and below.

Beads: Blanket stitch is a great stitch for incorporating beads, and with two rows, there are twice as many places to add beads. This stitch can also be a surface filling if using row after row of overlapping blanket stitches.

Here's How: Come up at A, loop thread down to right, string one bead, enter fabric at B and exit at C. Repeat across. Stitch another row, beginning a little below and to the left of first row.

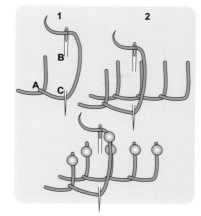

122 Long-and-Short Blanket

Skill Level: Easy

Description: Making the vertical length of the blanket stitches climb and fall creates a wavy line along the top edge of the stitch. Shortening the width of the stitch by half gives the shape more solidity.

Beads: Beads look great added to the bottom edge or the rising lines of this stitch. If you choose to put just one or two beads in the vertical section, they will tend to slide along the stitch unless you tack them in place.

Here's How: Come up at A, loop thread down to right, string one bead, enter fabric at B and exit at C. Repeat, varying the height of B so an undulating line is formed along top of the stitch.

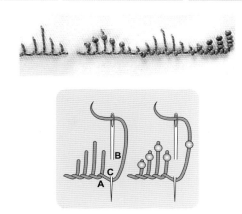

123 Slanted Blanket

Also known as slanting buttonhole and single feather.

Skill Level: Intermediate

Description: This #106 Blanket is worked so the vertical stitches are at a 45-degree angle to the horizontal stitch. In the example shown, the slanting stitches are alternately worked from one side and then the other, though the stitches can all be worked on one side as well.

Beads: This is a good stitch to add beads to when representing a branch or vine.

Here's How: Come up at A, string three beads and slide two down to fabric, loop thread down to right, enter fabric at B and exit at C. String three beads and slide two down to fabric, loop thread down to right, enter at D and exit at E. String three beads and slide two down to fabric, loop thread down to left, enter at F and exit at G. Repeat pattern, changing direction of slant every two stitches.

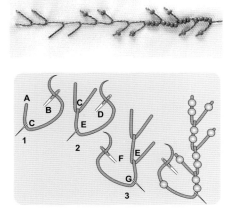

124 Picot Blanket

Also known as knotted blanket and knotted buttonhole.

Skill Level: Intermediate

Description: Making a blanket stitch with a knot at the top of the vertical stitch creates the picot in the stitch.

Beads: Beads in the knot accentuate the knot detail. This stitch looks nice worked in the long and short pattern with three beads in each picot.

Here's How: Come up at A, string three beads and slide two down to fabric, loop thread down to right and loop again as shown, enter fabric at B, exit at C and pull through, creating knot. Repeat.

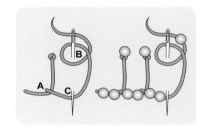

125 Two-Sided Blanket

Also known as double blanket and double buttonhole.

Skill Level: Easy

Description: Make one row of #106 Blanket, then turn the fabric around and work another row, slightly overlapping the space of the first row.

Beads: This stitch arrangement has a lot of possibilities. This example shows the second row overlapping the space in the first row, but it could actually go all the way to the horizontal part of the first row's stitches. Another option is to have them overlap vertical and horizontal lines. Beads take on a different look when worked in both stitches, creating a center line in the middle or borders along the edges.

Here's How: Come up at A, loop thread down to right, string one bead, enter fabric at B and exit at C. Repeat across. Rotate fabric and stitch another row, beginning a little below and to the left of first row.

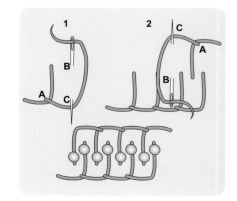

126 Grouped Blanket

Also known as spaced blanket and spaced buttonhole.

Skill Level: Easy

Description: This stitch is easy to make. Make one regularly-spaced blanket stitch, then make another stitch that is spaced very close to the first one, then repeat the process across the row.

Beads: Beads added to this stitch increase the impact of the stitch groupings. Make this stitch in groups of three stitches or any number, or alternate the groupings from two to four. It's a good, easy stitch for experimentation.

Here's How: Come up at A, loop thread down to right, string one bead, enter fabric at B and exit at C. Repeat across, making every other stitch closer together than the one before.

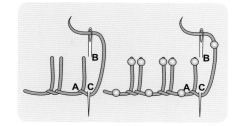

127 Feathered Blanket

Skill Level: Intermediate

Description: This stitch looks similar to #113 Double Feather, except that it is stitched with a tighter tension so the stitches are more angular and the turning corners are different.

Beads: Filling the base of this stitch with beads creates a straight line that zigzags across the pattern. Adding just one bead in the top part of the stitches accents the zigzag line.

Here's How: Come up at A, loop thread down to right, string one bead, enter fabric at B and exit at C. Repeat two more times. To change direction, hold thread up and to right, string one bead, enter fabric at D, exit at E, loop thread up to right, string one bead, enter at F and exit at G. Repeat two more times, then change direction again. Repeat across.

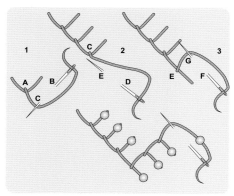

128 Embellished Feathered Blanket

Skill Level: Intermediate

Description: This is #127 Feathered Blanket with three straight stitches added to each inside corner, embellishing the stitch.

Beads: This example shows beads added to the straight stitches, but another option is to fill the blanket stitch part of the pattern with beads.

Here's How: Stitch a row of #127 Feathered Blanket stitch. Come up at A, string two beads, enter fabric at B, exit at C, string two beads, enter at D, exit at E, string two beads and enter at F. Repeat in each V-shape of #127.

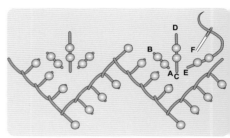

129 Wave Blanket

Skill Level: Easy

Description: Draw any winding line on fabric and make the blanket stitches meander anywhere you choose along the line.

Beads: Spacing these stitches a little closer together than basic blanket stitch adds more color to the pattern. Beads look great added to either section of the stitch.

Here's How: Come up at A, loop thread down to right, string two beads and slide one bead down to fabric, enter fabric at B and exit at C. Repeat, tilting slant of stitches to create a wavy line and adding one bead to some stitches and two beads to others.

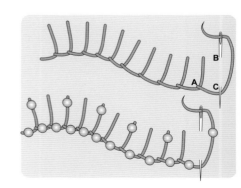

130 Fanned Buttonhole

Skill Level: Intermediate

Description: This stitch is basically blanket stitches worked in a semicircle with a straight stitch at the beginning to finish the fan shape.

Beads: Beads work better in the outside part of the stitches, since the inner "wheel" is too close at the center to accommodate the beads and individual beads slide along the stitch.

Here's How: Come up at A, enter fabric at B, exit at C, string one bead and slide it down to fabric, loop thread up to right, enter at D and exit at E. Repeat, slanting each stitch to create fan pattern.

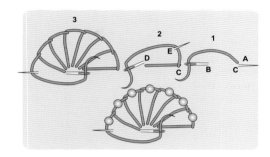

131 Lazy Daisy Buttonhole

Also known as detached chain blanket.

Skill Level: Intermediate

Description: Detached chain stitches dot the tops of this otherwise basic blanket stitch.

Beads: This stitch is the best for having fun adding beads. Make a garden of flowers by changing the beads used in each stitch, adding several to the tacking stitch of the chain stitch, or filling the looped section with beads.

Here's How: Come up at A, loop thread down to right, enter fabric at B and exit at C. Repeat across. Come up at the top of first stitch, enter fabric at top of stitch, exit about ¼" above, loop thread to right and under needle, pull through to create loop, string one to two beads and enter fabric above end of bead(s). Repeat at top of each stitch.

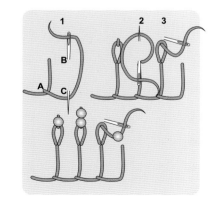

132 Overlapping Chevron

Skill Level: Intermediate

Description: By stitching an overlapping row of chevron stitches offset from the initial row, the center V-shapes change to diamonds or X's.

Beads: When adding individual beads to the center sections of this stitch, either be content with the fact that they will slide randomly along the stitch, or tack down the intersections of the stitches to corral the beads into permanent locations.

Here's How: Come up and make a small horizontal stitch, exit at center of stitch with thread below needle (A), string one bead, enter at B, exit at C, enter at D and exit at E with thread above needle. Repeat B through E parallel with first stitch and with thread below needle on last half of stitch using no beads. Repeat across. Stitch another row over the first row in the spaces between stitches.

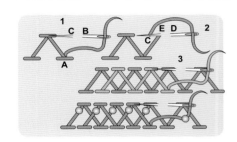

133 Slanted Cretan

Skill Level: Easy

Description: This stretched-out form of #109 Cretan presents an airy, sparce stitch.

Beads: Add beads to the small section of the stitch caught by the next stitch or in the larger section. The beads tend to stay in place in this stitch.

Here's How: Come up at A, string one bead, enter fabric at B, exit at C, string one bead, enter at D, exit at E, string one bead, enter at F and exit at G. Repeat B through G across.

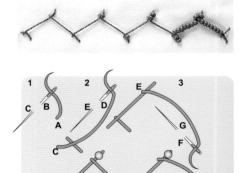

134 Lazy Daisy Cretan

Skill Level: Intermediate

Description: Adding detached chain stitches to the ends of an open cretan stitch adds a nice detail to the stitch pattern.

Beads: This pattern looks great embellished with beads. Use the suggestions for #131 Lazy Daisy Buttonhole for this stitch.

Here's How: Come up at A, loop thread down to right, enter fabric at B, exit at C, loop thread up to right, enter at D and exit at E. Repeat across. Come up at the top of the first stitch, enter fabric at top of stitch, exit about ¼" above, loop thread to right and under needle, pull through to create loop, string one to two beads and enter fabric above end of bead(s). Repeat at top of each upper stitch.

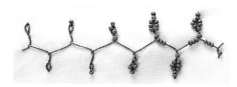

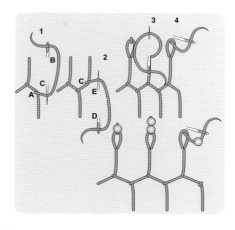

135 Lazy Daisy Leaf

Skill Level: Intermediate

Description: Detached chain stitches work well as leaf shapes. Placing three stitches together creates a small plant or leaf shape.

Beads: Add beads to make this stitch look like a leaf, a small plant (add a small flower bead), or part of a meandering vine.

Here's How: Come up at A, enter fabric at B, exit at C, loop thread to right and under needle, pull through to create loop, string two beads and enter fabric above end of beads. Repeat, making smaller loops on either side of first loop and using one bead instead of two.

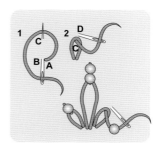

136 Lazy Daisy Flower

Skill Level: Intermediate

Description: Another arrangement of detached chain stitches, this is a radiating circle of long and short detached chain stitches that create a flower shape.

Beads: This is a great example of how beads can enhance a design. This example shows beads in the tacking stitch of the detached chains, making each petal longer and more colorful, with a seed bead placed in the center.

Here's How: Come up at A, enter fabric at B, exit at C, loop thread to right and under needle, pull through to create loop, string two beads and enter fabric above end of beads. Repeat, making four large loops radiating from center at right-angles. Make smaller loops between large loops using one bead instead of two.

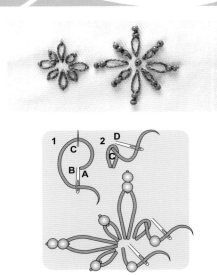

137 Fan

Skill Level: Intermediate

Description: Resembling #130 Fanned Buttonhole stitch, straight stitches and backstitches create a fan shape with pointed fans.

Beads: If placing beads in the points of the fans, use smaller beads or make the whole fan shape large enough to fit the beads. This example shows two stitch points replaced with single stitches across the outer edge of the fan shape. The beads create an effect similar to the pointed version.

Here's How: Come up at A, enter fabric at B, exit at C, enter at D and exit at E. Repeat straight stitches to form semicircle. Come up at top of second stitch, string one bead, enter fabric at top of first stitch and exit at top of third stitch. Repeat backstitch around ends of stitches, adding one bead to each stitch.

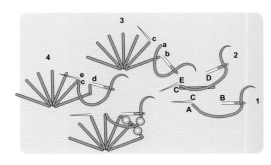

138 Feather

Also known as double feather and triple feather.

Skill Level: Easy

Description: This stitch is made of open U-shaped loops, each beginning at the base of the previous loop and offset from loop to loop.

Beads: This is the same as #112 Feather in freeform embroidery, yet this beaded section shows a completely different way to embellish the stitch.

Here's How: Come up at A, string two beads and slide them down to fabric, enter fabric at B, exit at C, string two beads and slide them down to fabric, enter at D, exit at E, string two beads and slide them down to fabric, enter at F and exit at G. Repeat D through G.

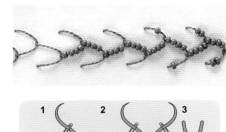

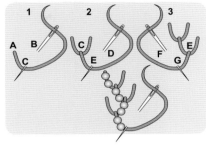

139 Feather Vine

Skill Level: Intermediate

Description: This is #112 Feather that is stitched on one side for several loops, then switched and stitched on the other side of several loops, creating a zigzag pattern.

Beads: Adding beads to one direction of the stitches adds a strong diagonal repeat to the pattern.

Here's How: Come up at A, string four beads and slide two down to fabric, enter fabric at B and exit at C. Repeat three more times. *String four beads and slide two down to fabric, enter at D and exit at E. Repeat from asterisk three more times. Repeat full pattern.

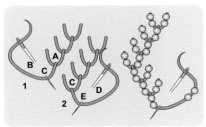

140 Flowered Feather

Skill Level: Intermediate

Description: This interesting stitch is made of lazy daisy stitches linked together with long tacking stitches in a zigzag pattern.

Beads: Adding beads can emphasize the stem or leaf shapes of this pattern.

Here's How: Come up at A, enter fabric at B, exit at C, loop thread to right and under needle, pull through to create loop, string three beads, enter at D, exit at E, enter at F, exit at G, loop thread to left and under needle, pull through to create loop and string three beads. Continue, alternating direction of loops and beaded straight stitches.

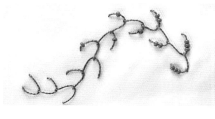

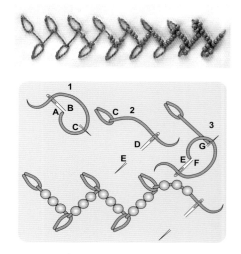

141 Meandering Feather

Skill Level: Easy

Description: This feather stitch creates a wave pattern by tilting each stitch to follow an imaginary curving line.

Beads: This lacy stitch is a great flower or leaf vine, with the beads as the leaves or flower buds.

Here's How: Come up at A, string one bead, enter fabric at B, exit at C, string one bead, enter at D and exit at E. Repeat B through E, changing the direction of stitch slightly each time to create gentle wave pattern.

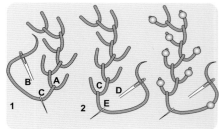

142 Herringbone

Skill Level: Easy

Description: Overlapping diagonal stitches form this crisscross pattern that is the basis for the following ornate patterns.

Beads: Beads can be sparse or dense in this easy pattern.

Here's How: Come up at A, string two beads, enter fabric at B, exit at C, string one bead, enter at D, exit at E and pull stitch through, positioning finished stitch on either side of two beads in previous stitch. Repeat B through E.

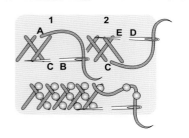

143 Herringbone and Blossoms

Skill Level: Intermediate

Description: After completing one row of #142 Herringbone, tack down the intersections with vertical stitches, then stitch the flower pattern made of three lazy daisy stitches at every other intersection.

Beads: Beads play a key role in this design, defining the flower shape as different from the unbeaded leaf shape. The two beads on the herringbone part of the stitch add further detail.

Here's How: Work #142 Herringbone, stringing two beads for each stitch and keeping each pair of beads at end of each stitch (1). Tack each stitch intersection in place with a small vertical stitch (2). Make three #93 Lazy Daisy stitches at every other lower intersection. Make one vertical above the intersection with four beads in the loop (3a) and one in the tack stitch (3b). Make one horizontal on either side of the intersection with no beads (4).

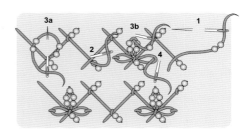

144 Herringbone and Leaves

Skill Level: Intermediate

Description: After completing one row of herringbone stitch, tack down the thread intersections with a small vertical stitch, then add a lazy daisy stitch in each upside down V shape.

Beads: Place a single bead in the end of every stitch to give this stitch a stronger horizontal border.

Here's How: Work #142 Herringbone, stringing two beads for each stitch and sliding one bead down to the fabric so there is one bead at each end of each stitch (1). Tack each stitch intersection in place with a small vertical stitch (2). Make #93 Lazy Daisy stitch below every upper intersection (3a and 3b).

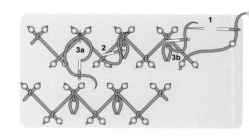

145 Overlapping Herringbone

Skill Level: Intermediate

Description: After completing one row of elongated herringbone stitch, stitch another row on top of the first, offset by half, then tack each intersection down with a small vertical stitch.

Beads: This example shows beads added to both the tacking stitches and the lines of the herringbone stitch.

Here's How: Work #142 Herringbone, stringing two beads for each stitch and sliding both beads into the center of each stitch as it is pulled in place (1). Work a second row of herringbone, stringing two beads for each stitch and alternately sliding the groups of beads to one end or the other of the intersections of the two rows of stitches so groupings create diamonds (2). Tack all intersections in place with small vertical stitches, stringing one bead before completing all the tacking stitches along the center intersections (3).

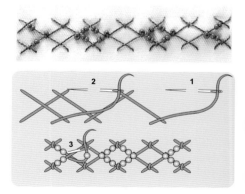

146 Twisted Herringbone

Skill Level: Intermediate

Description: In this version of herringbone, the diagonal stitches are twisted with the stitch before, creating a strong division from the center and edge parts of the stitch.

Beads: The beads are sure to stay in place with this strong division of stitch sections.

Here's How: Come up at A, string one bead, enter fabric at B, exit at C, string one bead and slide it down to fabric, slide needle under thread as shown (a), string four beads, enter at D and exit at E. *Slide three beads toward twist in thread, string one bead and slide it down to the fabric, slide needle under thread as shown (a), catching the three beads in center of long stitch, the fourth bead at end of previous stitch and the new bead at the beginning of the new stitch. String four beads, enter at E and exit at F. Repeat from asterisk.

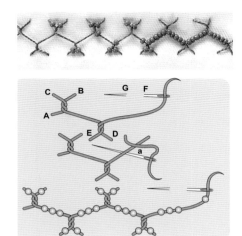

147 Rosette

Skill Level: Intermediate

Description: Make this charming little stitch by pushing the needle in and out of the fabric, wrapping the thread around the needle twice to create the shape, then pulling the needle through and tacking it in place.

Beads: Beads have the best effect in this stitch when added symmetrically.

Here's How: Come up at A, string 20 beads, enter fabric at B, exit at C, slide three beads down to fabric, wrap thread around tip of needle so first three beads are on one side of needle, slide three more beads to other side of needle and wrap thread around base of needle. Slide seven beads down, wrap thread around tip of needle and slide last seven beads down. Holding beads in place, pull needle through. Tack loops at top (4) and bottom (5).

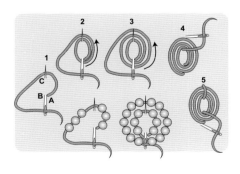

148 Rosette Vine

Skill Level: Intermediate

Description: This composition is made of a winding vine of chain stitches, with rosettes along the chain, and detached chains on the ends of the rosette with three straight stitches at the end.

Beads: This example shows beads placed only in the rosettes, making them into a branch of pomegranets.

Here's How: Stitch #147 Rosette (1 and 2). At the top of the rosette, make a #93 Lazy Daisy (3) and add three straight stitches at the end (4). Make a #92 Chain stitch with curving stem (5).

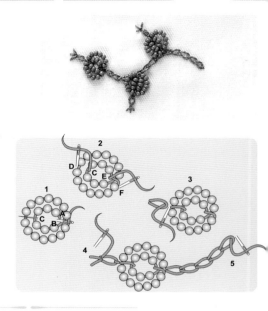

149 Rosettes in a Row

Skill Level: Intermediate

Description: This little row of posies is made of straight stitched flower stems with detached chain leaves and rossette flowers.

Beads: Fill the greenery or the flowers with beads.

Here's How: Stitch #147 Rosette, adding two beads to the top tacking stitch. Make a long stitch below for a stem. Make a #93 Lazy Daisy stitch for a leaf along the stem.

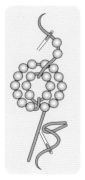

Smocking

Smocking is sometimes embellished with beads, but it is unusual to see beads used in the actual smocking stitches. Here are some basic stitches showing beads added to various parts of the stitch. When adding beads to stitches that span between pleats, the width of the bead or beads determines how much the pleat spreads open in the finished smocking, so there are limits on how many beads you can use between pleats. The samples were stitched using size 8 pearl cotton with sizes 8 and 11 beads on a thin, cotton fabric that was stitched with running stitches ¼" apart and then gathered. All stitches are worked from left to right, except #156 Van Dyke stitch, which starts on the right and is worked to the left.

150 Stem

Also known as outline.

Skill Level: Easy

Description: Take a backstitch in each fold of the fabric, working from left to right. When this stitch is worked with the thread below the needle, it is called stem stitch. When it is worked with the thread above the needle, it is called outline stitch.

Beads: The example shows one size 11 bead, then two size 11 beads, then one size 8 bead in each stitch. Notice how the pairs of size 11 beads spread the pleats in the fabric.

Here's How: Come up on left side of first pleat, string one bead and take a small stitch in the next pleat from right to left with the thread below the needle. Repeat across.

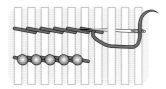

151 Cable

Skill Level: Easy

Description: Take a backstitch in each fold of the fabric, working from left to right, and alternating the thread above and below the needle. This creates stitches that alternately curve up and down across the row.

Beads: Add beads to every other stitch so they sit on either the top or the bottom curving stitches. Another option is to add beads in every stitch. The more beads used in the stitch, the more the pleat spreads apart. You can alternate the number of beads as shown in the lower row on the left side where every other lower stitch has three size 11 beads, and all the rest have one size 11 bead.

Here's How: Come up on left side of first pleat. *String one bead. Working right to left, take a small stitch in next pleat with the thread below the

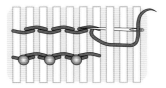

needle and then take a small stitch in next pleat with the thread above the needle. Repeat from asterisk.

---

152 Double Cable

Skill Level: Easy

Description: This is two rows of cable stitch, arranged so the first row begins with the stitch leaning to the top and the second row has the first stitch leaning to the bottom, creating a mirror image of the stitch pattern.

Beads: If adding beads to both of the center stitches that line up together, space the two rows apart enough to accommodate the beads, as shown in the lower example.

Here's How: Come up on left side of first pleat. *String one bead. Working right to left, take a small stitch in the next pleat with the thread above the needle and then take a small stitch in the next pleat with the thread below the needle. Repeat from asterisk across the row. To begin the next row, come up on left side of first pleat. *String

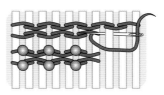

one bead. Take a small stitch in the next pleat with the thread below the needle and then take a small stitch in the next pleat with the thread above the needle. Repeat from asterisk.

153 Wave

Skill Level: Intermediate

Description: Create this wavy pattern by making #150 Stem stitches diagonally in one direction, then working in the other direction, making outline stitches. It it the basis for several pattern stitches such as trellis stitch.

Beads: Add beads to the turning point in each "wave" or in every stitch, determining the finished width of the pleats.

Here's How: Come up on left side of first pleat. String one bead. Working right to left, take a small stitch in next pleat with thread below needle and repeat three more times with each stitch a little above the previous stitch. Work the same stitch four more times with the thread above the needle, making each stitch a little lower than the previous one.

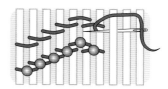

154 Trellis

Skill Level: Intermediate

Description: This stitch has several variations, all of which are made from two or more rows of #153 Wave stitch worked in a mirror image, creating a diamond pattern.

Beads: The example shows the same bead treatment as #153 Wave stitch, though another option is to add beads only on the bottom or top row for a different effect.

Here's How: Come up on left side of first pleat. String one bead. Working right to left, take a small stitch in next pleat with thread below needle. Repeat three more times with each stitch a little above the previous stitch. Work the same stitch five more times with the thread above the needle, making each stitch a little lower than the previous one. Come up on left side of second pleat below previous row. String one bead. Take a small stitch in next pleat from right with thread above needle. Repeat two more times with each stitch a little

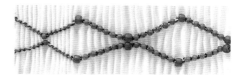

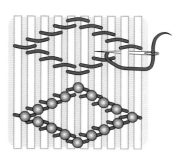

below previous stitch. Work same stitch four more times with thread below needle, beginning below last stitch and then with each stitch above the one before.

155 Feather

Skill Level: Intermediate

Description: This is a version of #113 Double Feather and #139 Feather Vine stitches, just stitched over the folds of the pleats.

Beads: Beads create a big impact when used in this stitch, especially if mixing large and small beads or placing more than two beads in each stitch.

Here's How: Come up on left side of first pleat. *String two beads. Take a small upward slanting diagonal stitch in same pleat ⅛" down, passing under loop created as you pull thread through and positioning one bead on either side of thread. String one bead. Repeat stitch. Repeat from asterisk two more times. Make three of the same stitches in the opposite direction and then reverse direction again.

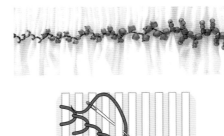

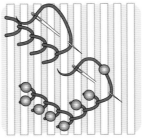

156 Van Dyke

Skill Level: Intermediate

Description: To make this stitch, take backstitches through two folds at once, then move up the left fold in the pair and take a horizontal stitch through that fold and the next fold to the left. Take a backstitch in the same place, then move down the left fold in the pair and take a horizontal stitch through that fold and the next one to the left. Repeat the whole process all across the row.

Beads: This is a small, tight stitch that opens up with larger beads in the backstitches.

Here's How: Come up on left side of the second pleat from the right. Working right to left, pass through the first and second pleat. *Move about ¼" up and pass through the second and third pleat. String one bead and pass through it again in the same place. Move back down ¼" and pass through

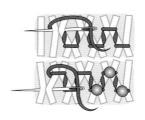

the third and fourth pleat. String one bead and pass through it again in the same place. Repeat from asterisk.

157 Diamond

Skill Level: Intermediate

Description: This stitch is made of two rows of #90 Chevron stitch worked across the pleats in a mirror image of each other, creating a diamond pattern across the fabric.

Beads: Using large beads in the backstitches of this pattern accentuates the pattern. If using beads in both of the stitches that meet in the center of the pattern, space the rows apart a little to accommodate the beads sizes.

Here's How: Come up on left side of first pleat. *Working right to left, pass through next pleat with thread below needle, string one bead, move up ¼" and pass through third pleat from right to left. Pass through fourth pleat with thread above needle, string one bead, move down ¼" and pass through fifth pleat. Repeat from asterisk. Work another row below the first, beginning with thread above needle and moving down ¼" for first part of pattern (a mirror image of first row).

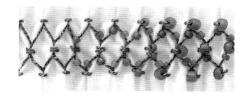

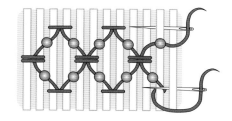

158 Crossed Diamond

Skill Level: Intermediate

Description: This pattern is made of two rows of #90 Chevron stitch, but the stitches are worked on top of each other, offset by two pleat folds, creating a small diamond shape with horizontal lines above and below.

Beads: This example shows beads added sparingly and then added in two colors, filling the stitches.

Here's How: Come up on left side of first pleat. *String one bead. Working right to left, pass through next pleat with thread below needle. Move up ¼" and pass through third pleat. String one bead and pass through fourth pleat with thread above needle. Move down ¼" and pass through fifth pleat. Repeat from asterisk. Work another row over the first, beginning with thread above needle

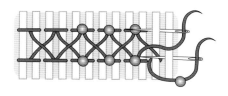

parallel to top of stitching and moving down ¼" for first part of pattern.

159 Surface Honeycomb

Skill Level: Intermediate

Description: The surface version of #160 Honeycomb stitch passes up and down from stitch to stitch on the front side of the fabric and resembles a larger version of #156 Van Dyke stitch.

Beads: Add beads to any part of this stitch.

Here's How: Come up on left side of first pleat. *String one bead. Working right to left, pass through next pleat with thread above needle. Move down ¼". and pass through same pleat. String one bead, pass through next pleat with thread below needle. Move up ¼" and pass through same pleat. Repeat from asterisk.

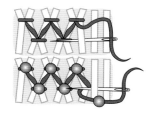

160 Honeycomb

Skill Level: Intermediate

Description: This stitch cinches two pleat folds together, then passes alternately up and down, behind the fabric to the next set of pleats, binding them together.

Beads: Stitch beads into one of the stitches at each intersection.

Here's How: Come up on left side of first pleat. *String one bead. Working right to left, pass through first and second pleat with thread above needle. Insert needle into right side of fold of second pleat, exiting on left side of same pleat down ¼". String one bead, pass through second and third pleat with thread below needle. Insert needle into right side of fold of third pleat, exiting on left side of same pleat up ¼". This pleat becomes first in pattern sequence. Repeat from asterisk.

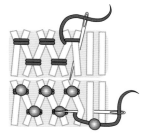

161 Stacked Triangle 162 Stacked Diamond 163 Stacked Heart

Skill Level: Intermediate

Description: These next three stitches are usually made of cable stitches stacked in a solid pattern to form the desired shape, but when adding beads, cable stitch would become a less dense pattern. These stitches are shown in stem and outline stitches worked symmetrically to create the patterns.

Beads: Beads are added to every stitch to create the three patterns.

Here's How (#161): Make one repeat of #153 Wave. Make two more smaller wave patterns, filling in the space below the first one, so that a triangle shape is formed.

Here's How (#162): Make one repeat of #153 Wave with three stitches on each side, plus the top center stitch. Make two smaller wave stitches below with two stitches and then one stitch on each side below center top stitch. Make a stitch below all the center stitches for the bottom point of the diamond shape.

Here's How (#163): Work two rows of #153 Wave, beginning with one stitch on right side, top turning stitch, two stitches down next side, bottom turning stitch, two stitches up next side, top turning stitch and one stitch down last side. Work next row, beginning under first stitch in previous row, making four stitches down, bottom turning stitch, three stitches up next side and turning stitch. Begin next row under second stitch of previous row, making three stitches down, bottom turning stitch, two stitches up next side and turning stitch. Make one more stitch under center of heart-shape with thread below needle.

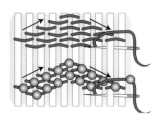
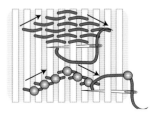
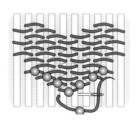

Ribbonwork

Ribbon embroiderers often use beads as accents to their stitching, but beads traditionally haven't been added to the ribbon stitches. I used size 8 beads for the following stitches. With the different sizes of needles, ribbon and thread for ribbon embroidery, it is easy to find lots of embellishment ideas for adding beads to this technique.

164 Running

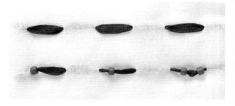

Skill Level: Easy

Description: Simple stitches in any direction can be worked in ribbon the same as any other embroidery thread. Here, they are shown as running stitches in a row.

Beads: Beads added to this stitch tend to crimp the ribbon most of the time, making a narrower stitch than when worked without beads.

Here's How: Come up, string one bead, enter fabric desired stitch width away and exit a short distance away, usually the same width or shorter than the stitch. Repeat across.

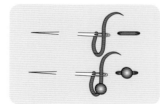

165 Ribbon Straight

Also known as Japanese ribbon.

Skill Level: Easy

Description: This is always a fun stitch to work in ribbon embroidery because it has such a unique effect. To make the stitch, come out of the fabric where you want the stitch to begin, then lay the ribbon flat. Pierce the ribbon with the needle where you want the stitch to end. Pull the ribbon through, being careful at the end to pull gently. The amount you pull the stitch determines the finished shape. Ideally, the stitch is pulled just enough so the sides near the end of the stitch curl over, creating a point. If pulled too much, the whole ribbon will curl into a narrow band. If not pulled enough, the stitch won't have a point.

Beads: Beads can be added to this stitch in several ways; string the bead and leave it up near the needle, so when piercing the ribbon and pulling through, the bead is caught at the end of the stitch. Another option is to slide the bead down to the beginning of the stitch or near the beginning.

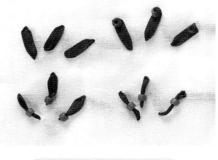

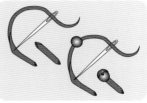

Here's How: Come up, string one bead and lay ribbon flat, piercing ribbon when entering fabric desired stitch width away. Pull through.

166 Couching

Skill Level: Easy

Description: Work this stitch with two strands of ribbon; lay one flat on the fabric and take small vertical stitches at regular intervals with the other, holding the first ribbon in place, gathering it slightly. Don't pierce the first ribbon with the second; just stitch around it.

Beads: Because this example shows large size 8 beads to couch this ribbon down, the base ribbon doesn't gather, creating a different effect than the unbeaded version described above. It's not necessary to use ribbon for the small stitches, so using a smaller bead and beading thread to couch the ribbon in place will create a gathered effect.

Here's How: Come up, string number of beads desired and lay ribbon flat on fabric in direction of stitch. With a new length of thread, come up behind center of first ribbon about ½" along first ribbon length, entering fabric in same place catching ribbon in stitch, but not piercing ribbon.

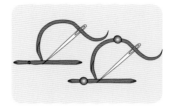

Repeat along ribbon, sliding beads along first ribbon and between stitches of second ribbon. Add a bead to the couching stitch, if desired.

167 French Knot

Skill Level: Intermediate

Description: These classic knots are the same version used in freeform embroidery (#115). Use the ribbon to make them loose or tight for different effects in designs.

Beads: Add beads before or after wrapping the ribbon around the needle for this stitch. If sliding the bead down to the fabric, wrapping the needle, then finishing the stitch, as in the middle example, the bead tends to lay so the hole shows. If stringing the bead, leaving it up near the needle, then wrapping the stitch as shown on the right, the bead tends to lay sideways.

Here's How: Come up, string one bead, wrap ribbon around needle as shown and insert needle in fabric close to ribbon, holding wrap as you pull through.

168 French Knot Variation

Also known as pistil.

Skill Level: Intermediate

Description: This is the same as a standard #115 French Knot, but enter the fabric at the end of the stitch a little distance away, usually from ¼" to ½", creating a long stitch connected to the knot.

Beads: Add beads to any part of this stitch to add color and texture to the design.

Here's How: Come up, string one bead, wrap ribbon around needle as shown and insert needle ½" or more away, holding wrap as you pull through.

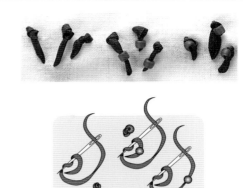

169 Cross

Skill Level: Easy

Description: These little bow-shaped stitches are simple cross stitches with a horizontal tacking stitch over the center intersection.

Beads: Add beads to the cross of this stitch or to the tacking stitch.

Here's How: Come up, enter fabric about ⅜" diagonally up to right and exit down ⅜". Enter fabric ⅜" diagonally up to left and exit under center intersection of stitches, coming out from behind stitches to right without piercing ribbon stitches. String one to three beads and enter fabric on other side of center intersection under ribbon, cinching first two stitches as you pull through.

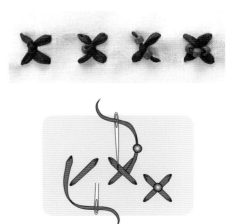

170 Fly

Skill Level: Easy

Description: This is the same stitch as #111 Fly stitch in freeform embroidery. Make a loop and tack it down with a small vertical stitch, making a V-shape.

Beads: Beads work well in this stitch. Add several beads to the tacking stitch, making it longer, or keep it short and the beads will stand out from the surface in an arch.

Here's How: Come up, loop ribbon down to right, enter fabric about ½" to right and exit about ½" below, centered between forming stitch. Pull ribbon through, forming a V-shape. String one bead, enter fabric below bottom of V, making a small vertical stitch.

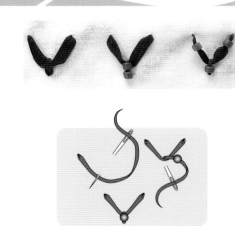

171 Lazy Daisy

Skill Level: Easy

Description: This is the same stitch as #93 Lazy Daisy worked in freeform embroidery and added to several of the crazy quilt stitches. Use the same ribbon for the small tacking stitch, or use a thread or contrasting colored or width ribbon.

Beads: Adding beads to the tacking stitch or the ribbon loop changes the look of the stitch a great deal.

Here's How: Come up, loop ribbon around to right, enter fabric in almost same place as beginning and exit about ½" away. Pull ribbon through, forming looped stitch. String one bead and enter fabric above loop.

172 Lazy Daisy Variation

Skill Level: Easy

Description: This is a detached chain stitch with an elongated tacking stitch to hold the loop in place.

Beads: Adding beads to the long tacking stitch creates a stamen for a flower. Use the beads to determine the length of the stitch or use smaller beads with beading thread for the tacking part of the stitch.

Here's How: Make the same as #171 Lazy Daisy, except string three beads instead of one and enter fabric at end of length of beads.

173 Plume

Skill Level: Easy

Description: Fold the ribbon into a loop and pierce the needle through the ribbon near the base of the loop, piercing two layers of ribbon. This creates a small gathered effect at the base of the loop.

Beads: Notice how different this stitch looks from the middle example to the example on the right. To achieve the look in the middle example, leave the beads up near the needle so they get caught in the part of the stitch that pierces the ribbon. To achieve the look in the example on the right, slide the beads down to the top of the loop, then complete the stitch.

Here's How: Come up and string one bead. Making sure ribbon isn't twisted, pierce ribbon near beginning and pass back into fabric. Pull through until loop is about ½" long.

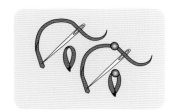

174 Cretan

Skill Level: Easy

Description: This basic Cretan stitch takes on a slightly different look when worked in ribbon. The stitch is easily made with alternating vertical stitches catching the previous stitch in the process.

Beads: Add beads to any part of this stitch.

Here's How: Come up, loop ribbon down to right, string one bead and slide it down to fabric, enter fabric diagonally about ½" up to right and exit about ¼" down. String one bead and slide it down to fabric, enter fabric diagonally about ½" down to right and exit about ¼" up. Repeat across.

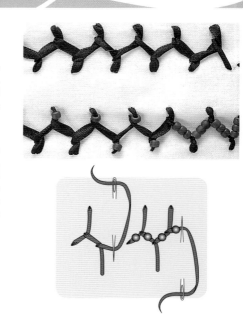

175 Sheaf

Skill Level: Easy

Description: This is three vertical straight stitches cinched together at the center with a small horizontal tacking stitch.

Beads: Beads can be added to any part of this stitch. Because the ribbon is thick, you don't have the same problem of scale that you do when adding beads to a thread worked in #100 Sheaf stitch.

Here's How: Make three ½"-long vertical straight stitches, spaced about ¼" from each other. Come up from back of center stitch, pass under stitches to left without piercing them. String one bead, pass into fabric under center stitch again, enter behind stitches from right side and cinch vertical stitches tight as you pull through.

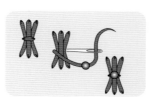

Beadwork Stitches

Beadwork stitches can greatly enhance embroidery. They can act as inserts between fabrics or ribbons, and can be as structural as in the Vintage Ribbon Bag on page 00 or can be appliquéd to projects either as the main piece or as an accent. The following are the most commonly used stitches shown on Aida cloth. Although you can work them on any fabric, Aida cloth works well with the size beads used for the sample. The samples in this section were made using 14-count Aida cloth, size B beading thread, a bead embroidery needle, and size 11 seed beads.

176 Peyote

Also known as gourd.

Skill Level: Intermediate

Description: This quick-to-work stitch is accomplished by stringing a bead, then passing through the next bead on the previous row, creating a bead pattern that resembles brickwork on its side.

Beads: Work stitch in any size seed bead, keeping in mind that the varying sizes will create slightly different looks, and larger beads will add weight to that section of the finished piece.

Here's How: To work this stitch on the Aida cloth, first stitch a bead over every other canvas thread in running stitch. Then pass through the last stitch on the back side of the fabric, pass up through the hole next to the last bead strung, pass through the last bead strung toward the end of the row, and begin peyote stitch, as shown.

At the end of the row, string another bead and work back the other way, passing through the beads in the previous row.

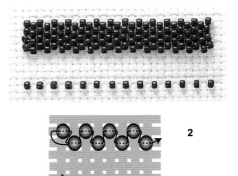

To attach the beadwork to the fabric along the sides, come up through the hole next to the bead and continue with the next row. To leave the sides of the beadwork open, pass through the beads as shown to position the needle for the next row.

Continue working in this manner until the beadwork is finished, then stitch the last row down to the fabric with running stitch or backstitch.

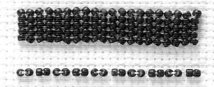

177 Brick

Also known as Comanche.

Skill Level: Intermediate

Description: In this firm, sturdy stitch, the beads are perpendicular to the rows of stitching and the finished beadwork looks like brickwork.

Beads: Work stitch in any size seed bead, keeping in mind that the varying sizes will create slightly different looks, and larger beads will add weight to that section of the finished piece.

Here's How: Row 1: String two beads, pass down two holes away and back up through one hole away. Pass up through the second bead strung, pulling the thread so the beads are side by side and perpendicular to the fabric. *String one bead, pass down through the next hole in the Aida cloth and up through the previous hole, passing up through the last bead strung. Repeat from the asterisk across the row. Row 2: String two beads, pass through the thread between the last two beads in row 1. Pass up through the last bead strung, pull the thread so the beads sit side by side. *String one bead, pass through the thread holding the next bead in place on row 1. Pass back up through the last bead strung. Repeat from asterisk to the end of the row. Repeat row two or three times or as many times necessary for the size of the beadwork desired. Stitch the last row down to the fabric, stitching through every loop of thread.

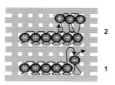

178 Herringbone

Also known as Ndebele.

Skill Level: Intermediate

Description: This stitch resembles herringbone fabric because the beads tilt opposite each other in columns. It is a very fast stitch because you add two beads at a time, instead of one. At first, however, it's a little challenging because the needle doesn't pass through in the place that common sense says it would for each stitch.

Beads: Work stitch in any size seed bead, keeping in mind that the varying sizes will create slightly different looks, and larger beads will add weight to that section of the finished piece.

Here's How: Row 1: String two beads, pass down through the next hole and back up the hole after that. Repeat the pattern across the row, except on the last stitch come up the hole between the two beads and up through the last bead in the row, instead of just coming up the next hole away.

Row 2: String two beads, pass through the next two beads in the previous row. Repeat across except for the last two beads, pass under the loop between the last two beads in the row, then pass back up through the last bead in the current row.

Repeat Row 2 until beaded band is as large as desired, then tack the last row down to the cloth.

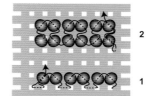

179 Right-Angle Weave

Skill Level: Advanced

Description: This interesting stitch is challenging at first because the thread passes through the beads in a figure eight path that takes a little while to understand. But once you are comfortable with the stitch, you will enjoy the rhythm and fluid drape of the finished beadwork.

Beads: Work stitch in any size seed bead, keeping in mind that the varying sizes will create slightly different looks, and larger beads will add weight to that section of the finished piece.

Here's How: Stitch a bead over every other canvas thread in running stitch. Pass up through the hole just before the last bead. Follow the pattern in the illustration to complete the band of beadwork, then tack the last row down at the topmost bead of each pattern repeat across the Aida cloth.

180 Netting

Skill Level: Intermediate

Description: Netting is made of loops of beads stitched together to form a net pattern. If you know how to stitch in peyote stitch, netting is the same concept, just with more beads in each stitch. The netting pattern can be made of any size loops of beads. The example was made using a three-bead pattern repeat.

Beads: Work stitch in any size seed bead, keeping in mind that the varying sizes will create slightly different looks, and larger beads will add weight to that section of the finished piece.

Here's How: String five beads, pass through the third hole away in the Aida cloth and back up the next hole. Pass back through the last bead strung. *String four beads, pass through the second hole away and back up through the next hole and through the last bead strung. Repeat from asterisk across. Working in the opposite direction, pass through the next bead. Follow the pattern in the illustration, stringing three beads and then passing through the center bead of the loop in the previous row and tacking the end of each row to the Aida cloth. Tack the last row down at the center bead of each three-bead loop across the Aida cloth.

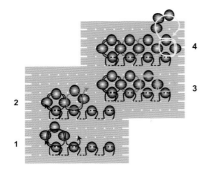

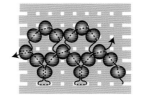

Elements for Flowers

Bead flowers are fun additions to embroidery. They make great accents in small projects, but can also be wonderful ornate pieces used as the main design element in a larger project. Because there are so many ways to make flowers with beads, you can get very creative exploring the possibilities with different shaped beads. But if you just want a quick and easy embellishment, there are lots of pressed glass flower and leaf shapes that can be the perfect addition to your embroidery creation. These samples were stitched on cotton gabardine with size B beading thread, a size 11 beading needle and a variety of bead shapes and sizes.

181 Stamens

Skill Level: Easy

Description: Stamens, the center part of the flower, are made by stringing the stem and flower beads, then stringing the beads you want as your stamen, then passing back through the flower bead and stem beads. It often helps to hold the stamen beads while pulling the thread to help snug up the thread and beads. This can be varied in several ways.

Beads: Work stitch in any size seed and pressed glass beads (or other accent beads) keeping in mind that the varying sizes will create slightly different looks, and larger beads will add weight to that section of the finished piece.

Here's How: To achieve the look in the first example, string three size 15 beads for the stamen, skip the last bead strung and pass back through the first two beads, and then the flower and stem beads. This creates a straight simple stamen.

Make it longer by adding more beads before the turnaround, or have the last bead strung be a larger size 11 bead or drop bead as in the second example. Repeat the process if desired to create several stamens in the flower.

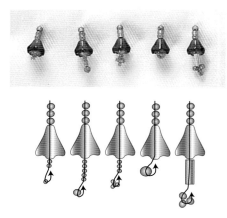

The third example is the result of skipping three beads in the turnaround; a nice symmetrical ending. To work this arrangement, hold the middle bead of the three beads while pulling the thread through the beads.

To achieve the look in the fourth example, use one large size 8 bead and pass back through the flower and stem.

To achieve the look in the last example, use bugle beads for the long part of the stamen and three size 11 beads for the turnaround section.

182 Hanging and Stationary Flowers

Skill Level: Easy

Description: In addition to deciding what the stamens will look like, decide if the flowers should hang from the fabric so they dangle, or be attached to the fabric so they stay in one place. Flower beads can have either center-drilled or side-drilled holes.

Beads: Work stitch in any size seed and pressed glass beads (or other accent beads) keeping in mind that the varying sizes will create slightly different looks, and larger beads will add weight to that section of the finished piece.

Here's How: Side-drilled flowers are easy to attach snugly to the fabric since the string goes through the flower, then back down through the fabric to hold the bead in place. If the flower has a tapered shape in the back, it's helpful to string a size 11 bead before and after the flower to get the flower to face directly away from the fabric and not lean to one side too much. To get these side-drilled flowers to hang, treat them as the turnaround bead in a dangle. To do this, string the stem beads, a larger bead (such as a size 8 bead), about three small size 15 beads, the flower bead, three more size 15 beads, then pass back through the large size 8 bead and stem beads. Hold the flower bead while pulling the thread through so it fits snugly in place.

Center-drilled flowers are easy to make into hanging beads because they are treated as one bead in a dangle. String the stem beads, the center-drilled flower bead, and the turnaround bead or beads, then skip the turnaround beads and pass back through the flower and stem beads. To make the center-drilled bead stationary, make a straight stitch: string the stem beads, the center-drilled flower bead, and the stamen, then pass back down into the fabric. Be sure to string enough stamen beads to reach from the center of the flower to the fabric.

To make bundles or branches of flowers, pass up through a part of the stem of a finished flower, then string a few more beads for the next flower stem, the flower bead and the turnaround bead or beads, and pass back down through the flower bead and the stem beads, all the way back to the fabric. Repeat this several times to create a branch filled with flowers.

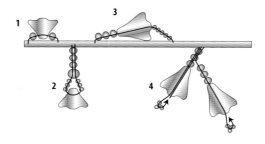

183 Flower Buds

Skill Level: Easy

Description: Make flower buds from stem beads and a larger bead to represent the bud of the flower.

Beads: Work stitch in any size seed and pressed glass beads (or other accent beads) keeping in mind that the varying sizes will create slightly different looks, and larger beads will add weight to that section of the finished piece.

Here's How: Stitch the same as the center-drilled flower beads described in #182 Hanging and Stationary Flowers, using size 11 or 15 beads for the stem and stamen, and a size 8 or 6 bead in place of the flower bead. Another way to make a flower bud is to use a drop bead. String several size 11 or 15 seed beads and then string three or more

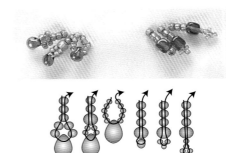

turnaround beads, the middle one being the drop bead, and pass back through the stem beads. You can also string a strand of beads with the drop bead in the center of the strand, then pass back down through the fabric by the first bead, creating a small loop.

184 Building Flowers from Several Beads

Skill Level: Easy

Description: You can make flowers from almost any type of bead. Finding which arrangement works for your project is half the fun.

Beads: Work stitch in any size seed and pressed glass beads (or other accent beads) keeping in mind that the varying sizes will create slightly different looks, and larger beads will add weight to that section of the finished piece.

Here's How: To make a daisy-shaped flower using side-drilled beads, string the number of beads desired for the flower, usually five to eight. Pass through the first several beads strung again, creating a circle of beads. Pass down through the fabric near the last bead and take a small stitch between each bead, catching the thread holding them together to anchor the flower. You then have the option of adding beads to the center of your flower or adding stems or leaves.

For hanging bead flowers, experiment with different sizes and shapes of beads for the different flower parts. The stem section can gradually increase in size, or you can use a disk bead just before the flower. For the flower itself, you can choose from many different pressed glass flower beads or use round beads for flower buds. Finally, the stamen can be anything from one bead to several hanging strands.

185 Attaching Leaves

Skill Level: Easy

Description: Pressed glass leaves can be attached to fabric in several ways. The method you use will partly be determined by the direction and placement of the hole in the bead.

Beads: Work stitch in any size seed and pressed glass beads (or other accent beads) keeping in mind that the varying sizes will create slightly different looks, and larger beads will add weight to that section of the finished piece.

Here's How: Center-drilled leaf beads can be stitched onto fabric with a simple straight stitch, or with several beads at the base and one at the top, creating a stem. Or they can be attached as in #182 Hanging and Stationary Flowers.

Side-drilled leaves that have the hole passing from the front of the bead to the back of the bead can't be simply stitched to the fabric by themselves without the thread showing, which can work if the thread is decorative, but not if it is beading thread. To attach these beads to fabric, string the leaf bead, then a smaller bead such as the size 11 bead in the example, then pass back through the leaf bead so the small bead holds the leaf bead in place. Another

method is to string the leaf bead and enough small beads to loop over the leaf bead and reach the fabric, then pass down through the fabric. This creates a small loop that holds the leaf in place. The last method is to make a hanging leaf in the same method as the hanging flowers, where the leaf is the center turnaround bead in the stitch.

Side-drilled leaves that have the hole passing from side to side at the base of the leaf can be stitched to the fabric by themselves with a simple straight stitch. The straight stitch can also be bordered by several small beads such as the size 11 beads in the example, creating a leaf-hanging-from-a-branch effect. Finally, they can also be attached as hanging flowers, where the leaf is the center turnaround bead in the stitch.

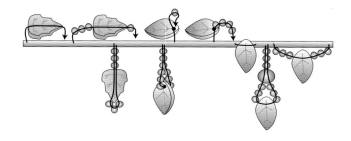

186 Seed Bead Leaves

Skill Level: Intermediate

Description: Seed bead leaves are leaf designs made of small beads embroidered in a leaf shape. There are two basic ways to make them.

Beads: Work stitch in any size seed bead, keeping in mind that the varying sizes will create slightly different looks, and larger beads will add weight to that section of the finished piece.

Here's How: One way to make leaves is to satin stitch or straight stitch beads onto the fabric in the shape of a leaf; this can be simply four or five stitches worked at an angle. A variation of this is to stitch a center line and make symmetrical diagonal lines of beads, radiating out from the center line, which can be an actual straight stitch of beads, or can be a drawn line on the fabric.

The second method is to string six beads, skip the last bead strung, pass through the next bead, string three beads and pass through the first bead and the fabric; this creates a small, freestanding leaf. Variations to this method include attaching the end to the fabric so the leaf lays flat or to making a straight stitch with six beads, coming back up through the fabric just before the fifth bead, passing through it toward the beginning of the strand, stringing three beads and passing through the first bead and the fabric.

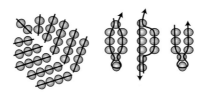

187 Seed Bead Flowers

Skill Level: Intermediate

Description: Seed bead flowers can be just as varied as the beads available. Here are several basic flower shapes.

Beads: Work stitch in any size seed bead, keeping in mind that the varying sizes will create slightly different looks, and larger beads will add weight to that section of the finished piece.

Here's How: The top three flowers are actually made in the same way, with slight variations. For the flower on the left, stitch a size 8 bead where you want the center of the flower to be, then make small looped backstitches around the size 8 bead with size 15 beads. The first four loops closest to the size 8 bead have three beads each. The next round of six loops have five beads each. Slightly overlap the loops or begin and end them next to each other to create a circle of loops.

The center top flower, worked all in size 15 beads, begins with three three-bead seed stitches work closely together for the center of the flower. Continue with five-bead loops, slightly overlapping the loops, until the flower is the size desired. The example has thirteen five-bead loops.

The small flower on the right begins with a size 8 seed bead straight stitched for the center of the flower, then five five-bead loops in size 15 beads

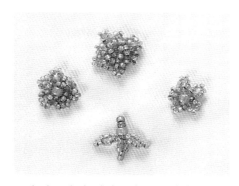

are backstitched side-by-side around the size 8 bead.

The last flower is made by stringing two size 11 beads, one size 8 bead, six size 15 beads, then taking a small stitch in the fabric where you want the center petal of the flower to end. Pass through the last two beads strung, string three size 15 beads, and pass through the size 15 bead just before the size 8 bead, pass through the size 8 bead, and the two size 11 beads. Take a small stitch in the fabric and pass back through the size 11 beads and the size 8 bead. Repeat the size 15 bead pattern for the two side petals to complete the design. This flower can also be made hanging by making the petals in the same manner as the second leaf pattern on the previous page.

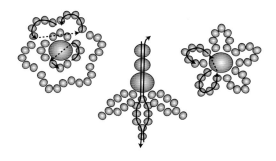

Fringes and Edgings

Fringes and edgings can be simple utilitarian stitches that hold two pieces of fabric together, or they can be elaborate, decorative elements in a design. An easy fringe worked in beautiful decorative beads can be the focal point of a simple project, elevating it to an elegant finished design. Generally, I classify edgings as short and narrow additions of beadwork and fringes as longer borders made of rows of dangles of beads. Edgings are usually sturdy, making them good choices for attaching two pieces of fabric together, as well as being decorative. Most fringes need a looser stitching tension than edgings so the dangles will hang and sway. If you use a tight tension, you may find that your dangles are stiff and might even stick out at odd angles, rather than hanging and moving in a fluid manner. This might be desirable for some effects, but in most cases, you will want your fringe to hang loosely. The samples in this section were stitched with a variety of bead sizes and types, using a size 11 beading needle, size B beading thread and stitched on the fold of quilters cotton fabric.

188 One-Row Brick

Skill Level: Easy

Description: This is the beginning row in beadwork's brick stitch. The beads are attached so their holes are perpendicular to the fabric's edge and the thread shows as it travels from bead to bead. It is an excellent edging for attaching two pieces of fabric together because it is a tight, even stitch. The sample is made with size 8 beads.

Beads: Work stitch in any size seed bead, keeping in mind that the varying sizes will create slightly different looks, and larger beads will add weight to that section of the finished piece.

Here's How: Beginning with the thread coming out of the edge of the fabric, string two beads and

take a small stitch in the edge of the fabric about one bead-width away. Pass back up through the last bead strung. For the repeating pattern, string one bead, take a small stitch in the edge of the fabric about one bead-width away, and pass back through the last bead strung. Repeat all along the edge. At the end of the row, you may need to take a small stitch in the fabric beyond the last bead to keep that bead from tilting up toward the other beads. The thread will show on that last stitch, so try to find a thread that matches the bead color.

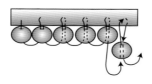

189 Picot Brick

Skill Level: Intermediate

Description: This nice picot edging is worked by making a single row of brick stitch, and then adding two more rows to create the picot edging. The sample is made with size 8 beads.

Beads: Work stitch in any size seed bead, keeping in mind that the varying sizes will create slightly different looks, and larger beads will add weight to that section of the finished piece.

Here's How: Row 1: Work a row of brick stitch as described in #188 One-Row Brick stitch, ending with the thread coming up through the last bead in the row. If you want the picots to be over the first row without any extra beads at the end of the row, be sure to string a multiple of three beads for the first row.

Row 2: *String two beads, skip one bead, pass down through the next bead, pass up through the next bead. Repeat from the asterisk across the row. Depending on how many beads are in the first row, you may not be able to go back up through a bead at the end of the row. Whichever place your thread ends, at the end of the row you need to pass in and out of adjacent beads so the thread is coming up out of the last bead in row 2.

Row 3: *String one bead, pass down through the next bead in row 2 and row 1, then up through the next bead in rows 1 and 2. Repeat across row 2 from asterisk, ending by adding the last bead and passing down through row 2 and row 1 to the fabric. Weave in end.

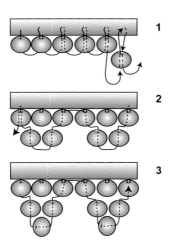

1

2

3

190 Peyote Edge

Skill Level: Easy

Description: This narrow edging of even count peyote stitch is easy to complete and is a great way to add a strip of color and texture to the edge of a piece. Make this band as thick or as thin as you choose. The sample is made with size 8 beads.

Beads: Work stitch in any size seed bead, keeping in mind that the varying sizes will create slightly different looks, and larger beads will add weight to that section of the finished piece.

Here's How: Row 1: Stitch beads along the edge of the fabric in running stitch, spacing the beads about a bead-width from each other. Pass back up through the fabric next to the last bead in the row. Turn.

Row 2: Pass back through the last bead in row 1, *string a bead and pass through the next bead in the row. Repeat from the asterisk across the row. Turn.

Row 3: String a bead and pass through the last bead in the previous row, *string a bead and pass through the next bead in the previous row. Repeat from the asterisk across the row.

Repeat row 3 once more, or until your edging is the thickness desired. Weave in end.

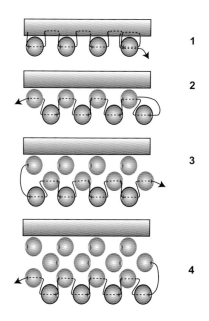

191 Herringbone

Skill Level: Intermediate

Description: Herringbone stitch is named for the visual effect created by the alternate tilting columns of beads which make up the stitch. It is actually easier to stitch when started on a foundation such as the edge of a piece of fabric, rather than stitched unattached. This edging of herringbone stitch ends with a little picot which is easy to achieve at the end of this stitch technique. The sample is made with size 8 beads.

Beads: Work stitch in any size seed bead, keeping in mind that the varying sizes will create slightly different looks, and larger beads will add weight to that section of the finished piece.

Here's How: Row 1: Make a running stitch across the edge of the fabric, stringing two beads in each stitch and making the stitches about two bead's width long. The beads will not lie flat. Pass back up through the last bead strung.

Row 2: String two beads and pass down through the next bead in the previous row, and back up through the next bead in the previous row. Repeat across the row, except for on the last stitch, string two beads and pass down through the last bead in the row to the fabric, taking a small stitch and passing back up through the last beads in the rows, ending up coming out the last bead in the just completed row.

Repeat row 2 once more, or until your edging is the length desired. For the final picot row, repeat row 2 stringing only one bead instead of two beads for each stitch, and weaving in the thread at the end of the row.

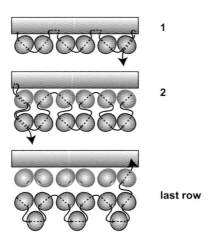

1

2

last row

192 Classic Edge

Skill Level: Easy

Description: This simple edging is one of the most commonly used edgings in beadwork. It is easy to work, though it is often challenging to keep the stitches evenly spaced. Each stitch needs to be about a bead-width away from the previous stitch so the beads line up evenly.

Beads: Work stitch in any size seed bead, keeping in mind that the varying sizes will create slightly different looks, and larger beads will add weight to that section of the finished piece. The sample is made with size 8 beads.

Here's How: Beginning with the thread coming out of the edge of the fabric, string three beads. Take a small stitch in the fabric about a bead-width away and pass back through the last bead strung, pull the stitch snug, so the first and third beads are perpendicular to the fabric and the second bead lies horizontally. *String two beads, take a small stitch in the fabric about a bead-width away and pass back up through the last bead strung. Repeat from the asterisk across the row. Weave in end.

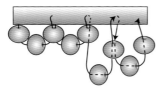

193 Classic Spaced Variation

Skill Level: Easy

Description: Spacing the beads a little farther apart and adding more beads changes the look of the classic edging. The look of this edging can be altered dramatically by changing the types of beads used, such as using a large drop bead in the center of each stitch.

Beads: Work stitch in any size seed bead, keeping in mind that the varying sizes will create slightly different looks, and larger beads will add weight to that section of the finished piece. The sample is made with size 8 beads.

Here's How: Beginning with the thread coming out of the edge of the fabric, string five beads. Take a small stitch in the fabric about three bead-widths away and pass back through the last bead strung, pull the stitch snug, so the first and last beads are perpendicular to the fabric and the middle three beads create the little arch. *String four beads, take a small stitch in the fabric about three bead-widths away and pass back up through the last bead strung. Repeat from the asterisk across the row. Weave in end.

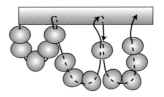

194 Shallow Loops

Skill Level: Easy

Description: Using classic edging and increasing the number of beads in each stitch and the space between stitches begins to form a row of loops scalloping across the edge of the fabric. Vary this stitch by making the stitches closer together, elongating the loops, or by adding more beads in each stitch.

Beads: Work stitch in any size seed bead, keeping in mind that the varying sizes will create slightly different looks, and larger beads will add weight to that section of the finished piece. The sample was made with size 8 seed beads. If using a different sized bead or number of beads per stitch, adjust the distance of the stitches.

Here's How: Beginning with the thread coming out of the edge of the fabric, string ten beads. Take a small stitch in the fabric about ½" away and pass back through the last bead strung, pulling the stitch snug, so the beads create an arch. Pull tightly so the edging is firm, or keep the tension loose so the edging is more fluid. *String nine beads, take a small stitch in the fabric about ½" away and pass back up through the last bead strung. Repeat from the asterisk across the row. Weave in end.

195 Two-Row Tapered Horizontal Netting

Skill Level: Intermediate

Description: Netting begins with #194 Shallow Loops. This stitch adds a second row.

Beads: Work stitch in any size seed bead, keeping in mind that the varying sizes will create slightly different looks, and larger beads will add weight to that section of the finished piece.

Here's How: Row 1: Follow the steps in stitch #194 Shallow Loops, but do not weave in the end. Leave the thread coming out of the last bead strung.

Row 2: Pass through the next four beads. *String seven beads, pass through the center bead in the next loop of beads in row 1. Repeat from the asterisk across the row. Weave in end.

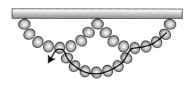

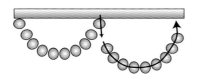

196 Tapered Three-Row Horizontal Netting

Skill Level: Intermediate

Description: This example shows an edging that builds on the previous two edgings, creating a three-tiered net that tapers from the edges.

Beads: Work stitch in any size seed bead, keeping in mind that the varying sizes will create slightly different looks, and larger beads will add weight to that section of the finished piece.

Here's How: Rows 1 and 2: Follow the steps #195 Two-Row Tapered Horizontal Netting. Pass through the remaining beads in row 1, take a small stitch through the fabric, and pass back up through the five beads in the end of row 1 and four beads in row 2. You will be just past the center of the last loop in row 2.

Row 3: *String seven beads, pass through the center bead in the next loop of beads in row 2. Repeat from the asterisk across the row. Weave in end.

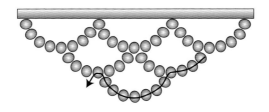

197 Horizontal Netting with Dangles

Skill Level: Advanced

Description: This variation of #196 Tapered Three-Row Horizontal Netting combines large and small beads for the netting with dangles added to the final edging, creating an undulating fringe design. Using different sized beads for the first three rows of netting simplifies the stitching because it's easier to see which bead to stitch through in each loop.

Beads: Work stitch in any size seed and leaf or accent beads, keeping in mind that the varying sizes will create slightly different looks, and larger beads will add weight to that section of the finished piece.

Here's How: Row 1: String one size 8 bead, two size 11 beads, one size 8 bead, two size 11 beads and one size 8 bead. Take a small stitch in the fabric about ¼" away and pass back through the last bead strung. *String two size 11 beads, one size 8 bead, two size 11 beads and one size 8 bead. Take a small stitch in the fabric about ¼" away and pass back through the last bead strung. Repeat from asterisk across the row. Turn to work in the opposite direction. Pass through the two size 11 beads and the next size 8 bead.

Row 2: *String two size 11 beads, one size 8 bead, two size 11 beads and pass through the size 8 bead in the center of the next loop on the previous row. Repeat from asterisk across the row. Pass down through beads at the end of the row to the fabric. Take a small stitch in the fabric. Turn to work in the opposite direction. Pass back up through the beads so you are through the size 8 bead in the end loop on the last row.

Row 3: Repeat row 2.

Row 4: String one size 6 bead, five size 11 beads, one size 6 bead, three size 11 beads, one leaf bead, three size 11 beads and pass back through the size 6 bead, the five size 11 beads and the size 6 bead. Pass through the beads in rows 3 and 2 as shown. String the short bead pattern and repeat, alternating long and short dangles across. Weave in end.

198 Classic Picot

Skill Level: Intermediate

Description: This is another common beadwork edging that works very well in embroidery. The picots can be made using many variations from drop beads to groups of beads.

Beads: Work stitch in any size seed bead, keeping in mind that the varying sizes will create slightly different looks, and larger beads will add weight to that section of the finished piece. The example was stitched in size 8 beads.

Here's How: String four beads, skip the last bead, pass back through the next bead. String two beads. Take a small stitch in the fabric ¼" away, pass back through the last bead strung. *String three beads, skip the last bead, pass back through the next bead. String two beads. Take a small stitch in the fabric ¼" away, pass back through the last bead strung. Repeat from asterisk across the fabric edge.

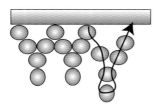

199 Classic Picot Crowded Variation

Skill Level: Intermediate

Description: This is a smaller, denser version of #199 Classic Picot, worked with one fewer bead in the repeat, and stitched very close together.

Beads: Work stitch in any size seed bead, keeping in mind that the varying sizes will create slightly different looks, and larger beads will add weight to that section of the finished piece.

Here's How: String three beads, skip the last bead, pass back through the next bead. String one bead. Take a small stitch in the fabric one bead's width away, pass back through the last bead strung. *String two beads, skip the last bead, pass back through the next bead. String one bead. Take a small stitch in the fabric one bead's width away, pass back through the last bead strung. Repeat from asterisk across the fabric edge.

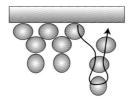

200 Classic Picot Bugle Bead Variation

Skill Level: Intermediate

Description: This variation of #198 Classic Picot shows what a difference a change of beads can make to a pattern.

Beads: Work stitch in any size seed and bugle beads, keeping in mind that the varying sizes will create slightly different looks, and larger beads will add weight to that section of the finished piece.

Here's How: String one size 8 bead, one bugle bead, one size 8 bead, and three size 11 beads, skip the size 11 beads, pass through the size 8 bead. String one bugle bead and one size 8 bead. Take a small stitch in the fabric ¼" away, pass back through the last bead strung. *String one bugle bead, one size 8 bead, and three size 11 beads, skip the size 11 beads, pass through the size 8 bead. String one bugle and one size 8 bead. Take a small stitch in the fabric ¼" away, pass back through the last bead strung. Repeat from asterisk across the fabric edge.

201 Overlapping Loops

Skill Level: Intermediate

Description: These modified backstitch loops can create a nice edging without a lot of work.

Beads: Work stitch in any size seed bead, keeping in mind that the varying sizes will create slightly different looks, and larger beads will add weight to that section of the finished piece.

Here's How: String 12 beads. Beginning ½" away, make a ¼"-long backstitch. String 12 beads. Beginning ½" away, make a backstitch that comes out of the fabric at the end of the first loop (about ¼"). Pass through the last bead in that loop. *String 11 beads, beginning ½" away, make a backstitch that comes out of the fabric at the end of the previous loop, pass through the last bead in the loop. Repeat from asterisk across the row.

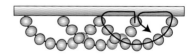

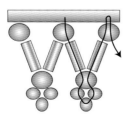

202 Overlapping Loops with Dagger Variation

Skill Level: Intermediate

Description: This variation of #201 Overlapping Loops uses smaller beads for the loops and dagger beads in the middle of the loops, creating a more delicate effect.

Beads: Work stitch in any size seed and drop beads, keeping in mind that the varying sizes will create slightly different looks, and larger beads will add weight to that section of the finished piece.

Here's How: String one size 8 bead, five size 11 beads, one dagger bead, five size 11 beads, one size 8 bead. Beginning ½" away, make a ¼"-long backstitch. String one size 8 bead, five size 11 beads, one dagger bead, five size 11 beads, one size 8 bead. Beginning ½" away, make a backstitch that comes out of the fabric at the end of the first loop. Pass through the last bead in that loop. *String five size 11 beads, one dagger bead, five size 11 beads, one size 8 bead, beginning ½" away, make a backstitch that comes out of the fabric at the end of the previous loop, pass through the last bead in the loop. Repeat from asterisk across the row.

203 Crowded Overlapping Loops on Curve

Skill Level: Intermediate

Description: Here, almost the same beads and stitch pattern as #202 Overlapping Loops with Dagger Variation creates a completely new look just by stitching the beads closely together. Working this same pattern on a straight edge of fabric will result in a ruffled edge.

Beads: Work stitch in any size seed and drop beads, keeping in mind that the varying sizes will create slightly different looks, and larger beads will add weight to that section of the finished piece.

Here's How: Stitch the same pattern as #202, except use only two size 11 beads instead of five, drop beads instead of dagger beads, and for the backstitches, instead of starting ½" away and making the stitch ¼"-long, start two bead's widths away and make the stitch one bead-width long. Gather the fabric before or after adding the bead edging.

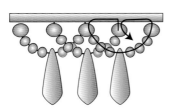

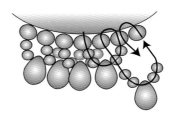

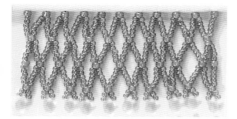

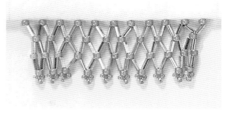

204 Vertical Netting

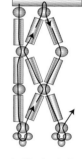

Skill Level: Intermediate

Description: Vertical netting is worked one dangle at a time, whereas horizontal netting is worked row by row. Vertical netting has a more fluid quality to the finished beadwork.

Beads: Work stitch in any size seed and drop beads, keeping in mind that the varying sizes will create slightly different looks, and larger beads will add weight to that section of the finished piece.

Here's How: String (one size 8 bead and five size 11 beads) three times, *string one size 8 bead, two size 11 beads, one drop bead, and two size 11 beads. Pass back through the last size 8 bead strung. String five size 11 beads, one size 8 bead, five size 11 beads. Skip the next size 8 bead on the previous strand, and pass through the next size 8 bead. String five size 11 beads, one size 8 bead, five size 11 beads. Take a small stitch in the fabric about ¼" away and pass back up through the last size 8 bead strung. String five size 11 beads, one size 8 bead, five size 11 beads. Pass through the size 8 bead skipped in the previous strand. String five size 11 beads. Repeat from the asterisk across the row, ending the row at a size 8 bead that enters the fabric.

205 Vertical Netting with Bugle Beads

Skill Level: Intermediate

Description: This is the same stitch as #204 Vertical Netting, but bugle beads replace the size 11 beads and three size 11 beads replace the drop beads bordered by size 11 beads. The bugle beads speed up the beading time, since you only have to string one bead instead of five for that step.

Beads: Work stitch in any size seed and bugle beads, keeping in mind that the varying sizes will create slightly different looks, and larger beads will add weight to that section of the finished piece.

Here's How: String (one size 8 bead and one bugle bead) three times, *string one size 8 bead and three size 11 beads. Pass back through the last size 8 bead strung. String one bugle bead, one size 8 bead, one bugle bead, skip the next size 8 bead on the previous strand, and pass through the next size 8 bead. String one bugle bead and one size 8 bead. Take a small stitch in the fabric about ¼" away and pass back up through the last size 8 bead strung. String one bugle bead, one size 8 bead, and one bugle bead. Pass through the size 8 bead skipped in previous strand. String one bugle bead. Repeat from the asterisk across the row, ending the row at the size 8 bead that enters the fabric.

206 Classic Dangle Fringe

Skill Level: Intermediate

Description: This most basic of fringes is what most fringes are built from. The trick to making this kind of fringe is to avoid piercing the thread that's already in the beads as you pass back up through the beads. One way to do this is to hold the thread taut on the table, so that you are less likely to pierce it. Another way is to snug the beads around your finger, just passing through a few at a time. Always check to see if you've pierced the thread by pulling the needle with the beads on it toward you before pulling the needle through the beads. If the beads slide easily up the thread, you know you haven't pierced it. Taking a small stitch in the fabric before passing to the next dangle location helps lock the beads in place so your tension stays even across the fringe. The sample is made with size 8 beads.

Beads: Work stitch in any size seed bead, keeping in mind that the varying sizes will create slightly different looks, and larger beads will add weight to that section of the finished piece.

Here's How: String 10 beads, skip the last bead and pass back through all the other beads, taking a small stitch in the fabric. Take a horizontal stitch in the fabric, coming out of the edge of the fabric about one bead's width away. Repeat the process all along the edge.

207 Classic Dangle Fringe Variation

Skill Level: Intermediate

Description: Taking #206 Classic Dangle Fringe and changing the sizes and types of beads can create an incredible selection of fringe designs that are limited only by your imagination. Here is a typical layout with small beads for the bulk of the dangle and larger beads accenting the top and bottom.

Beads: Work stitch in almost any size or type of beads, keeping in mind that varying sizes will create slightly different looks, and larger beads will add weight to that section of the finished piece.

Here's How: String one small faceted bead, 20 size 11 beads, one bugle bead, one small faceted bead, one size 6 bead and three size 11 beads. Skip the last three beads and pass back through all the other beads taking a small stitch in the fabric. Take a horizontal stitch in the fabric, coming out of the edge of the fabric about one bead's width away. Repeat the process all along the edge.

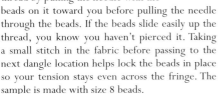

20

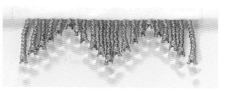

209 Zigzag Fringe Variation

Skill Level: Intermediate

Description: This variation of #206 Classic Dangle Fringe goes back to a simple fringe but plays with the number of beads in each dangle, creating an interesting zigzag wave pattern along the bottom edge.

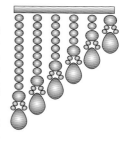

208 Classic Fringe with Swarovski Cube Detail

Skill Level: Intermediate

Description: Here is another variation on #206 Classic Dangle Fringe, using sparkly Swarovski cubes for an elegant presentation. Notice that the dangles are all identical except for the number of size 11 beads at the beginning. Varying the number of one type of bead in the dangles creates the undulating bottom edge.

Beads: Work stitch in almost any size or type of beads, keeping in mind that varying sizes will create slightly different looks, and larger beads will add weight to that section of the finished piece.

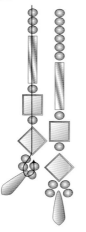

Here's How: String three size 11 beads, one long twisted bugle bead, one size 11 bead, one center-drilled cube, one size 11 bead, one diagonal drilled cube, two size 11 beads one dagger bead, two size 11 beads. Skip the last five beads and pass back through all the other beads taking a small stitch in the fabric. Take a horizontal stitch in the fabric, coming out of the edge of the fabric about ¼" away. Repeat the process all along the edge, alternately stringing six and then three size 11 seed beads at the beginning of the dangle.

Beads: Work stitch in any size seed and drop beads, keeping in mind varying sizes will create slightly different looks, and larger beads will add weight to that section of the finished piece.

Here's How: String 10 size 11 beads, one size 8 bead, two size 15 beads, one drop bead, two size 15 beads. Skip the last five beads strung and pass back through the other beads taking a small stitch in the fabric. Take a horizontal stitch in the fabric, coming out of the edge of the fabric about two bead's widths away. Repeat the process all along the edge decreasing the first size 11 beads by two beads for each successive dangle until you work one dangle beginning with the size 8 bead, then begin increasing size 11 beads until you are back up to ten. Repeat the zigzag pattern all across the edge.

211 Dangle Detail

Skill Level: Intermediate

Description: Sometimes you will need just a single dangle as a detail in your stitching. Here is a variation on #210's crystal pattern.

Beads: Work stitch in almost any size or type of beads, keeping in mind that varying sizes will create slightly different looks, and larger beads will add weight to that section of the finished piece.

Here's How: String one size 8 bead, one flower bead, one size 11, one diagonally drilled cube, one size 11 bead, one 8mm crystal, one size 11 bead, one 6mm crystal, one size 11 bead, one 5mm crystal, one size 15 bead, one 4mm crystal, one size 15 bead, one 3mm crystal, three size 15 beads. Skip the last three beads strung and pass back up through all the other beads.

210 Tapered Fringe Variation

Skill Level: Intermediate

Description: This version of #209 Zigzag Fringe Variation takes just one repeat of its gradually changing dangle lengths and adds gradually larger Swarovski crystals, ending in a flower bead.

Beads: Work stitch in almost any size or type of beads, keeping in mind that varying sizes create slightly different looks, and larger beads add weight to that section of the finished piece.

Here's How: String one size 6, 8 and 11 beads, (one bugle, one size 11) three times, one size 15 bead, one 3mm crystal, one size 15 bead, one 4mm crystal, one size 15 bead, one 5mm crystal, one size 15 bead, one size 15 bead, one 8mm crystal, one size 15 bead, one flower bead, three size 15 beads. Skip the last three beads and pass back up through all the other beads taking a small stitch and passing through fabric, spacing the dangles about ¼" from each other. Increase the first size 11 bead group to five, nine, 13, 17 and 21 beads, then reduce the number of beads in the same pattern.

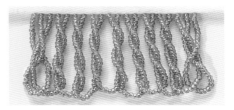

212 Classic Looped Fringe

Skill Level: Easy

Description: This technique creates a row of dangling loops that are easy to stitch.

Beads: Work stitch in any size seed bead, keeping in mind that the varying sizes will create slightly different looks, and larger beads will add weight to that section of the finished piece.

Here's How: String 50 size 11 beads, take a stitch about ⅛" away and come back out of the fabric ⅛" away. Repeat all along the edge.

213 Classic Twisted Looped Fringe

Skill Level: Easy

Description: This version of #212 Classic Looped Fringe is found on many beaded purses from the 1920s and before. The twisting links the individual fringes together and adds detail to the basic design.

Beads: Work stitch in any size seed bead, keeping in mind that the varying sizes will create slightly different looks, and larger beads will add weight to that section of the finished piece.

Here's How: String 50 size 11 beads, take ⅛"-long stitch, beginning about ⅛" away. *String 50 beads. Pass the needle under one side of the adjacent strand three times. Take ⅛"-long stitch in the edge beginning about ⅛" away. Repeat from asterisk all along the edge.

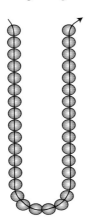

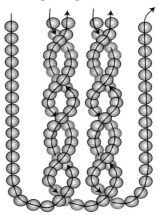

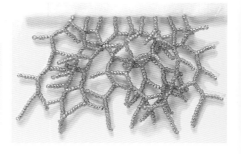

214 Classic Twisted Fringe

Skill Level: Intermediate

Description: This is a different way of twisting fringe than #213, and is based on #206 Classic Fringe in structure.

Beads: Work stitch in any size seed bead, keeping in mind that the varying sizes will create slightly different looks, and larger beads will add weight to that section of the finished piece.

Here's How: String 40 size 11 beads, one size 8 bead, one size 6 bead, and three size 15 beads. Skip the last three beads and pass through the size 6 and size 8 beads. String 40 beads and, continually holding the thread at the end of the beads, twist the strand either in your fingers, over your hand, or on your leg until the strand of beads kinks up on itself. Still pinching the strand at the end of the beads, take a small stitch in the fabric, holding the thread at the beads until you pull the last of the thread through. Take a horizontal stitch ¼" long and repeat the process for each dangle.

215 Branched Fringe

Skill Level: Intermediate

Description: This branching fringe is easier to make than it looks. It is very versatile as well. Use this stitch for an ocean coral look, for adding leaf beads, making leaves at the ends of the short stalks, or making wonderful hanging branches. The sample is stitched in size 11 beads.

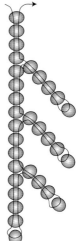

Beads: Work stitch in any size seed bead, keeping in mind that the varying sizes will create slightly different looks, and larger beads will add weight to that section of the finished piece.

Here's How: String 41 beads. Skip the last bead and pass through 10 beads. *String six beads, skip the last bead and pass through the next five beads and five more beads from the 41-bead section, working toward the fabric edge. Repeat from the asterisk five more times, passing into the fabric, then out again about ¼" away. Repeat the whole process for each branching fringe dangle.

Section 3: Projects

Here is a small sampling of the possibilities embroidering with beads has to offer. From simply stitching a few beads here and there to adding beads to established needlepoint and embroidery stitches, you will find new and different ideas for using beads in your stitching, as well as traditional bead embroidery techniques.

Blue Swirls and Stripes Pillow

This is an easy project that is a good introduction to beads and embroidery. The design depends on the fabric you choose. It needs to have an all-over pattern where you can pick out a repeating part to work your bead-embroidered stripes. I used a swirly pattern and made a winding stripe by stitching three beads at the ends of the curls in a meandering line. But you could also use this technique on a regular pattern, such as squares or a plaid, and tack your beads at the intersections of the lines for straight stripes across the fabric.

Finished Size

20" square pillow

Stitches Used

Backstitch

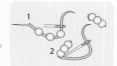

Figure 3-1

Tips for Success

If you are creating the stripes as you go from an all-over design as I did, it is easiest to start with the largest stripe across the center, or near the center of the design, and work the remaining stripes above and below.

You can stitch this project without putting the fabric in a hoop or frame. Just be sure to lay it flat on a table as you work and be careful not to pull the stitches so tightly that they pull and gather the fabric between stitches.

By taking the small stitch before moving to the next point in the pattern, you lock your beads in place, minimizing the possibility of the thread pulling on the back side of the fabric.

For a snug fit on a pillow, cut your fabric to the size of the pillow form and sew the pillow pieces together with a ½" seam. The pillow form will fit snugly in the pillow casing.

Materials

- 28 grams clear or blue size 8 seed beads
- Beading needle and thread to match fabric or beads
- 2 squares (20") printed fabric
- 20" square pillow form
- Sewing machine
- Basic sewing supplies

Instructions

1. Cut a 30" length of thread and thread the needle. Tie a knot at the tail end.

2. Working from right to left and beginning about 2" from any edge of one piece of fabric, come up with your needle from the back of the fabric at one of the points in the printed pattern which you have chosen to use to make your stripe.

3. String three beads and make a backstitch, passing down through the fabric about ⅛" to the right, and coming back up ⅛" to the left, where your thread first came out of the fabric, as in Figure 3-1 (1).

4. Take a small hidden stitch by passing down through the fabric next to your finished beaded stitch and back up again at the next point in the printed pattern for the next stitch (2).

5. Continue each stitch in the same manner, working across the fabric in a diagonal stripe (or any direction you choose), ending about 2" from the other edge of the fabric.

6. Secure the thread on the back of the fabric and repeat for another stripe about 5" from the first stripe.

Assembly

1. Pin the 20" fabric squares right sides together and sew a ½" seam along all the sides, leaving a 10" turn-hole opening along one side.

2. Clip the corners.

3. Turn right-side out and insert the pillow form.

4. Sew the turn-hole opening closed.

Green and Gold Notions Purse

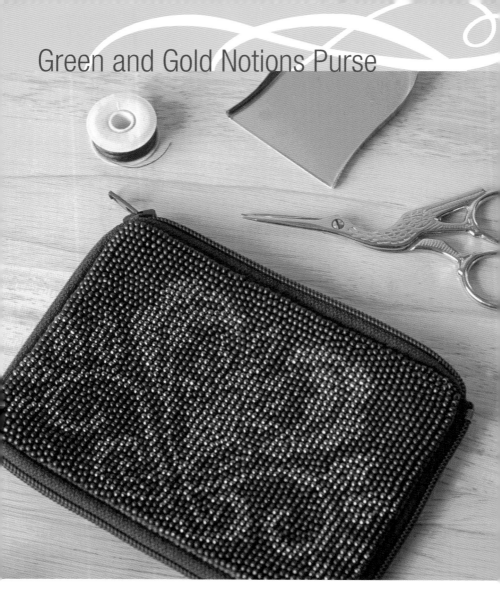

Take a basic needlepoint stitch pattern, work it in beads, and you will create a beautiful design with a wonderful glassy texture. Because the beads are more durable than threads, which so easily snag and can get dirty, you can just throw this purse in your bag and take it wherever you go.

Finished Size

3½" x 5" purse

Stitches Used

Tent

Tips for Success

All beads are different. Because the size of the beads I used was just a little bit large for the mesh size, I had to nudge some beads about to fit into place. Notice how the rows and columns don't line up exactly. I happen to like this movement in the pattern. But if this bothers you in your project, pass a length of thread through the beads diagonally across the grid to line them up better. Then, wet the design and pull it into shape; the beads will usually line up in a regular pattern.

Materials

* 20 grams green size 11 seed beads
* 14 grams bronze size 11 seed beads
* 2 skeins green six-strand embroidery floss to match purse or beads
* Bead embroidery needle
* 3½" x 5" purse that unzips all around and has 14-count mesh for needlepoint (46 x 64 holes)
* Optional: 2 pieces (6" x 4") lining fabric
* Basic sewing supplies

Instructions

1. Unzip the purse and unfold mesh edges so you can stitch all the way to the corners.

2. Using six strands of embroidery floss, stitch the outer perimeter of the mesh in tent stitch, as detailed on page 49, without any beads.

3. Using two strands of embroidery floss, stitch the pattern in tent stitch, following Figure 3-2, picking up one bead in the color indicated for each stitch in the chart.

Finishing

1. If the finished bag is warped, wet the whole piece and pull it into shape.

2. Stitch through the beads diagonally to ensure they line up vertically and horizontally (see Tips).

3. Let the purse is dry.

4. Turn under the raw edges of the two pieces of lining fabric, pin over the inside of each rectangle, and sew in place. Zip the purse closed.

■ green
□ bronze

Figure 3-2

Fringed Pillow

For this project, you can choose your own fabric, make a pillow and fringe it with beads, or speed up your project by using a purchased pillow and then adding the bead fringe. Whichever way you choose to make this project, have fun with the beads. You can use bead colors that pull from the colors in the pillow fabric, as I did, or you can contrast with your fabric, such as a black or red pillow with silver or gold beads.

Finished Size ❨❩
23" square pillow

Stitches Used ❨❩
Netted Fringe

Tips for Success ❨❩
For a snug fit on a pillow, cut your fabric to the size of the pillow form and sew the pillow pieces together with a ½" seam. The pillow form will fit snugly in the pillow casing.

Materials
* 2 hanks dark green size 11 seed beads
* 21 grams bronze size 11 seed beads
* 28 grams medium green size 8 seed beads
* 28 grams olive green size 6 seed beads
* 21 grams brown size 8 triangle beads
* 28 grams medium green size 5 triangle beads
* 144 amber small drop beads
* Beading needle and thread to match fabric or beads
* 2 squares (24") printed fabric to coordinate or contrast with beads
* 24" square pillow form
* Sewing machine, ironing board and iron
* Basic sewing supplies

Instructions

1. Pin the two square of fabric right sides together and sew along the sides with a ½" seam allowance, leaving about 12" turn-hole opening along one side.

2. Trim off the corners of the seam allowance close to the stitching.

3. Turn right-side out and press.

4. Attach a 30" length of beading thread to the corner, beginning along the side with the opening, and follow the fringe pattern, as shown in Figure 3-3 on the next page.

5. Complete the fringe pattern around the pillow casing, turning the corners as shown in Figure 3-4 on page 175.

6. Insert the pillow and sew the turn-hole opening closed.

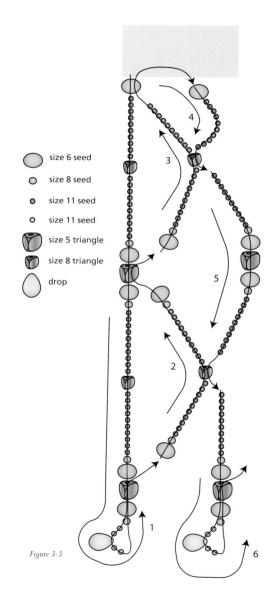

size 6 seed

size 8 seed

size 11 seed

size 11 seed

size 5 triangle

size 8 triangle

drop

Figure 3-3

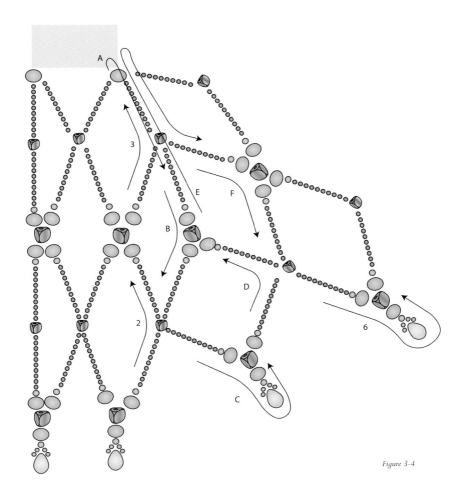

Figure 3-4

Grapevine Petit Container

This easy project shows the striking effect of just a few well-placed beads embroidered on fabric. The leaf and drop beads do all the work in the design; all you have to do is add a few lines of small seed beads to suggest the stems and curls of the grapevine and you are done.

Finished Size
1½" x 2" box

Stitches Used
Straight
Backstitch

Materials

- 1½" x 2" enamel box with lid
- 2½" square of fabric
- ⅝"-long leaf bead
- 12 purple ³⁄₁₆"-long drop beads
- 12 iridescent purple ⅛"-long drop beads
- 2 grams green size 11 seed beads
- 2 grams green size 15 seed beads
- Beading needle and thread to match fabric or beads
- Pencil
- Scissors

Instructions

1. Lightly trace the Figure 3-5 pattern on the fabric with pencil.

2. Use a 24" strand of thread and begin at the base of the stem to backstitch seven size 11 beads and the leaf, stitched to the fabric along the line with the green leaf in Figure 3-5.

3. Backstitch the size 15 beads over the curling vine lines.

4. Backstitch three size 11 beads for the stem of the grape cluster.

5. Straight stitch the purple drop beads in place by using a combination of the bead arrangements shown in Figure 3-6.

6. Weave in ends.

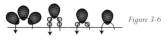

Figure 3-6

Assembly

Trim the fabric and mount in the box lid following the box manufacturer's instructions.

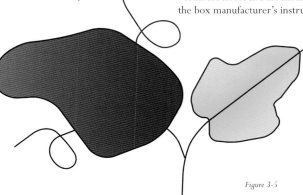

Figure 3-5

Wired Ribbon Beaded Blossom

Creating decorative flowers with beautiful wired ribbon is easy and fun. Adding beads to the ribbon makes your project even more stunning, and it's easy to do with simple edging stitches that highlight the colors in the ribbon, adding sparkle and texture to the design.

Finished Size

4" x 6" pin

Stitches Used

Fringe
Edging

Materials

- 14 grams rose size 11 seed beads
- 7 grams bronze size 15 seed beads
- 7 grams rootbeer size 15 seed beads
- 7 grams gold size 11 seed beads
- 14 grams salmon-lined green size 11 seed beads
- 15 green ¼"-long drop beads
- 15 rose size 8 seed beads
- Beading needle and thread to match ribbon or beads
- 2 yards 1½"-wide wire-edged silk ribbon with green along one edge and rose along the other
- Pin back
- Wire-cutting scissors
- Basic sewing supplies

Instructions

1. Cut the ribbon as follows:
   - three 11" lengths for the leaves
   - one 10" length for the inner blossom
   - one 14" length for the outer blossom

Leaves

1. Pull both ends of one wire along the rose colored edge of one 11" length of leaf ribbon, gathering the ribbon as much as you can.
2. Tie the wire in a knot to hold the gathers in place and cut, leaving about ¼" tails.
3. Fold the ribbon in half and stitch the gathered end together on the wrong side of the leaf.
4. Pinch the green side opposite the fold and fan out the green side forming the leaf shape.
5. Repeat steps 1 through 4 for the other two 11" lengths and set aside.

Blossoms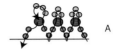

1. Pin the ends of the 10" inner blossom ribbon right sides together and backstitch together with ¼" seam allowance.

2. Pull both ends of the wire along the green-colored edge of the ribbon, gathering the ribbon as much as you can.

3. Tie the wire in a knot to hold the gathers in place and cut, leaving about ¼" tails.

4. Repeat steps 1 through 3 for the 14" outer blossom ribbon.

5. Using the beading thread and needle, stitch bead pattern A in Figure 3-7 to the inner blossom using the rootbeer, bronze and size 11 rose-colored beads. Stitch bead pattern B to the outer blossom using the size 11 rose-colored beads.

6. Work the fringe, as shown in Figure 3-8, on the gathered edge of the inner blossom using the remaining beads and spacing each dangle about ⅛" apart.

A

B

Figure 3-7

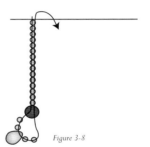

Figure 3-8

Assembly

1. Place the inner blossom with the center fringe in the middle of the outer blossom and stitch together along the gathered edges, gathering the opening closed as you go.

2. Arrange the leaves behind the flower so they extend about 1½" beyond the flower petals and stitch in place to the center bottom of the blossom.

3. Sew the pin back over the center back of the arrangement.

Ribbon-Embroidered Box

Ribbon embroidery is a fast and easy technique that is often enhanced by small accents of beads stitched as flower centers. Here, I used beads also as stems, flowers and parts of stitches to add more texture and interest to the design. It is easy to change the finished shape of this project by using a square or oval cardboard box and making the couched border follow the shape of the box lid.

Finished Size

5"-diameter box

Stitches Used

Backstitch
Lazy Daisy
Ribbon Straight
Stem
Couching

Materials

- 4 grams gold size 8 seed beads
- 4 grams copper aurora borealis size 11 seed beads
- 4 grams green size 15 seed beads
- ½"-long flower bead
- Size 8 green seed bead
- Size 6 green seed bead
- 3 bronze ⅛" drop beads
- 2 yards 7mm variegated peach-and-yellow silk ribbon
- 3 yards 7mm green silk ribbon
- 2 yards 4mm variegated yellow-and-green silk ribbon
- 1 yard light green 4mm silk ribbon

- ½-yard decorative gimp
- Beading needle and thread to match fabric or beads
- Chenille needles
- Tapestry needles
- 18" x 22" printed fabric
- 5"-diameter cardboard box with lid (painted desired color on inside and sides or covered with fabric)
- Thick white glue
- 5"-diameter circle batting
- Rubber band that fits around the box lid
- Pencil in contrasting color of fabric
- Basic sewing supplies

Instructions

1. Cut an 8" square from the printed fabric.
2. Lightly draw the basic lines of the design with pencil onto the center of the square.
3. Stitch the design, following Figure 3-9.

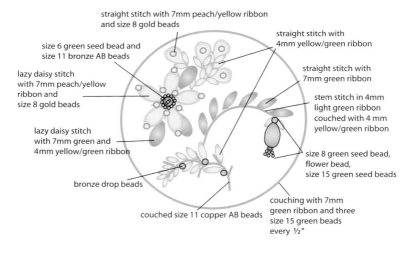

straight stitch with 7mm peach/yellow ribbon and size 8 gold beads

size 6 green seed bead and size 11 bronze AB beads

lazy daisy stitch with 7mm peach/yellow ribbon and size 8 gold beads

lazy daisy stitch with 7mm green and 4mm yellow/green ribbon

bronze drop beads

straight stitch with 4mm yellow/green ribbon

straight stitch with 7mm green ribbon

stem stitch in 4mm light green ribbon couched with 4 mm yellow/green ribbon

size 8 green seed bead, flower bead, size 15 green seed beads

couching with 7mm green ribbon and three size 15 green beads every ½"

couched size 11 copper AB beads

Figure 3-9

Assembly

1. Trim the fabric around the needlework to 1" from outer couched circle.

2. Place some glue on the top of the box lid and smooth to the edges.

3. Place the batting on the top of the glue on the box lid.

4. Smooth glue along the side of the box lid.

5. Center the needlework over the box lid and press the fabric into the glue along the side of the lid, pulling the fabric so the top is smooth and making sure it stays centered.

6. Put the rubber band around the side of the lid to hold the fabric in place as it dries. Let dry completely.

7. Trim excess fabric.

8. Cover the raw edge by gluing decorative gimp along the side of the lid.

Rainbow Square Box Lid

Small needlepoint stitch samplers like this one are fun to make because they work up quickly and are versatile enough to use in lots of different places. This one is glued to a box, but you could easily use it for the cover of a needlecase or zippered coin purse instead. The beads are quick embellishments that add to the established colors, and the beaded edging completes the design.

Finished Size
4" square box

Stitches Used
Tent
Rhodes
Scotch Variation
Byzantine
Straight

Materials

- 7 grams green size 8 seed beads
- 7 grams green size 11 seed beads
- 4 grams green size 15 seed beads
- 4 grams blue size 15 seed beads
- 4 green ⅝"-long leaf-shaped beads
- 4 pink ¼"-long drop beads
- Size 5 pearl cotton in colors, as follows:
  - cream
  - pale yellow
  - pale green
  - green
  - light turquoise
  - blue
  - dark blue
  - purple
  - plum
  - rose
  - pink
- Tapestry needle and thread
- Beading needle and thread to match beads
- 4" square 18-count canvas
- 4" square wooden box, varnished or painted
- Thick craft glue
- Ironing board and iron
- Basic sewing supplies

Instructions

1. Prepare the canvas by overcasting around the edges, so it won't fray while you are working.

2. Following the Figure 3-10 stitching chart, stitch the pattern on the canvas with the tapestry needle and pearl cotton.

3. Fold the unstitched edges of the canvas to the back of the work and baste in place.

4. Steam press the finished piece, pulling it square and pressing it flat. Let cool completely.

5. Sew the size 15 blue seed beads, leaf beads and drop beads in place on the top of the canvas at the dots indicated in figure 3-10.

6. Stitch the edging to the first unstitched row of canvas along the edges of the square, following the bead edging pattern shown in Figure 3-11.

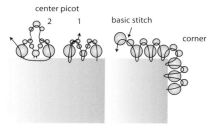

Figure 3-11

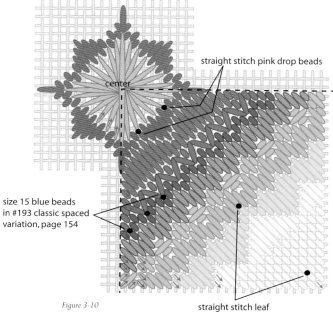

straight stitch pink drop beads

center

size 15 blue beads in #193 classic spaced variation, page 154

Figure 3-10

straight stitch leaf

Assembly

Glue the needlework to the top of the box.

Cabochon Pin

You might not consider pins to be bead embroidery, but cabochon projects are almost all created by stitching beads to a nonwoven fabric base using edging or beadwork stitches. This versatile pin can grace your jacket lapel or hold a special scarf in place. The color of beads you use will depend on the colors in your cabochon. It's easiest to pick a beautiful stone or glass cabochon and then pull colors from it when choosing the seed beads and accent beads for the piece.

Finished Size

1½" x 2", depending on size of cabochon

Stitches Used

Peyote
Edge

Materials

- 7 grams iridescent purple size 8 seed beads
- 7 grams iridescent pale blue size 11 seed beads
- 4 grams iridescent purple size 15 seed beads
- 4 grams pale green size 15 seed beads
- 6 orchid ⅛" drop beads
- ¼"-long iridescent drop crystal
- ³⁄₁₆"-long orchid faceted accent bead
- 1" to 1¼" cabochon

- Beading needle and thread to match fabric or beads
- 2" to 2½" scrap felt
- 2" to 2½" scrap Ultrasuede
- Craft glue
- Pen
- Pin back
- Basic sewing supplies

Instructions

Cabochon Cage

1. Place the cabochon on the felt and trace lightly around the cabochon shape with a pen.

2. Remove the cabochon and cut out the shape, cutting about ¹⁄₁₆" outside of the line so the felt is a little larger than the cabochon.

3. Repeat steps 1 and 2 with the Ultrasuede and set the Ultrasuede aside for assembly.

4. Work one row of the classic edging stitch with the size 8 seed beads, as in Figure 3-12, stitching on the pen line on the felt. When you reach the beginning, string one bead, pass down through the first bead strung, then back up through the last two beads strung.

5. Work two rows of peyote stitch using the size 11 seed beads, as in Figure 3-13, inserting the cabochon after the first round, and pulling the stitches tight so the cabochon is encased in the beading.

6. Work one round of peyote stitch with the green size 15 seed beads, alternately stringing one bead and then two beads for each stitch, as in Figure 3-14. Pull tightly as you go so the circle gets smaller and holds the cabochon more securely in place.

7. Weave in ends.

Embellishment

1. Attach a new length of thread, so you begin with the thread coming out of the bottom of one of the beads on the first round.

2. String two size 11 seed beads and pass down through the next bead on the first row, as in Figure 3-15. Repeat around.

3. String three size 11 seed beads and pass up through the next bead and down the bead after that, as in Figure 3-16. Repeat around twice so the three-bead edging is in and out of every bead on the first row.

4. Pass the needle and thread to one of the side size 8 beads to begin the dangling loops, as shown in Figure 3-17.

5. String enough beads to drape below the cabochon and pass through the size 8 bead on the other side of the cabochon. (Adjust the number of beads to fit your own piece.)

6. Pass through the size 8 seed beads as in Figure 3-17 and then string another loop that hangs a little lower than the first, making a dangle as shown.

7. Pass through the same bead on the opposite side.

8. Weave in ends.

o	size 15 seed, green
o	size 15 seed, pale blue
◯	size 11 seed, pale blue
⬤	size 8 seed, blue
◊	⅛"drop
⬭	½"large accent
⬙	⅜"-long accent

Bead Key

Figure 3-12

classic edging

Figure 3-13

size 11 peyote

Figure 3-14

size 15 peyote

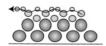

Figure 3-15

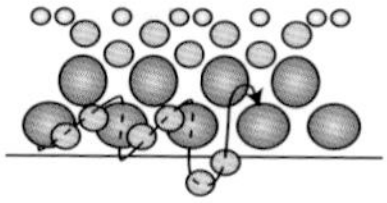

Figure 3-16

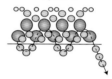

Figure 3-17

Assembly

1. Poke two holes in the Ultrasuede so the pin back fits through.
2. Glue the pin back and ultrasuede to the felt.

Sage and Snowflake Christmas Ornament

This Scandinavian-themed ornament uses bugle beads for the main design element with edging stitches and fringe dangles as tassels to finish off the design. Because it's made of two pieces of Aida cloth, it's a great piece to add a date or "made by" note in cross-stitch on the back side of the piece.

Finished Size

4" from point to point,
not including tassels or hanging loop

Stitches Used

Straight
Edge
Classic Fringe Dangles

Materials

- 7 grams cream ¼"-long bugle beads
- 4 grams silver size 11 seed beads
- 14 grams cream size 11 seed beads
- 8 iridescent clear size 8 triangle beads
- 12 flat ⅛"-diameter vintage clear faceted beads
- Beading needle and thread to match fabric and beads
- 2 squares (5") sage 18-count Aida cloth
- Ironing board and iron
- Basic sewing supplies

Instructions

1. Stitch the central pattern onto one 5" square of Aida cloth, following Figure 3-18.

2. Cross stitch or embroider the date or "made by" on the center of the other piece of Aida cloth, if desired.

Assembly

1. Turn the edges of each piece of Aida cloth under so the squares are 2⅞" wide, or 4" from point to point. Press in place.

2. Pin the two pieces of Aida cloth wrong sides together.

3. Sew Aida together along the edges.

Figure 3-18

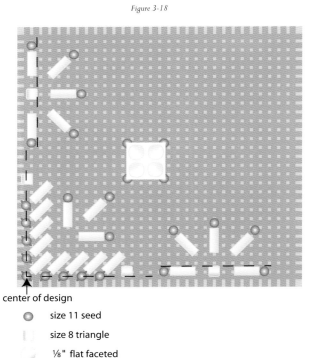

center of design

⬤	size 11 seed
	size 8 triangle
	⅛" flat faceted
	¼" bugle

Embellishment

1. Stitch the edging along all the sides of the ornament, as shown in Figure 3-19.

2. Attach a new length of thread at each corner and make a hanging loop at the top, a long tassel at the bottom and two medium tassels at each side corner.

3. Weave in ends.

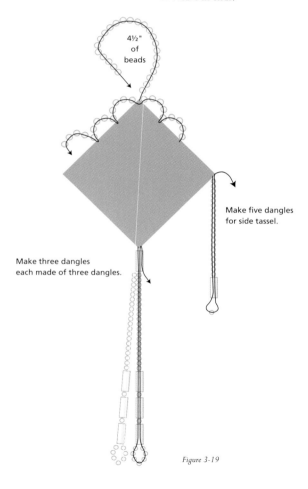

4½"
of
beads

Make five dangles
for side tassel.

Make three dangles
each made of three dangles.

Figure 3-19

Silver Star Christmas Treasure Bag

This little bag is great for hanging a small gift for someone special at the holidays, or anytime, since the colors are not tied to Christmas. In addition to the edging stitches in this project, you get to try the twisted fringe technique for the hanging chain, and twisted strands of beads — a different way to work with beads altogether.

Finished Size

2½" diameter, not including hanging chain

Stitches Used

Edging
Twisted Fringe
Twisted Strands

Materials

* 28 grams silver size 15 seed beads
* Beading needle and thread to match fabric or beads
* 2½" x 5" piece dark blue Ultrasuede
* Air-soluble tracing pencil
* Basic sewing supplies

Instructions

1. Use the Figure 3-26 pattern on page 201 to cut two 2¼" hexagons from the Ultrasuede.

2. Transfer the full-size points of the star design from Figure 3-26 on page 201 to one Ultrasuede hexagon piece using the air-soluble tracing pencil.

3. Bring needle and thread from back to front of hexagon where indicated to begin on Figure 3-20 and working counterclockwise, string on 36 seed beads, take a small stitch at the next star point, pass back through eight beads and string on 28 more seed beads.

4. Take a small stitch at the next star point, pass back through eight beads and string on 28 more seed beads. Repeat this step three more times.

5. When you reach the last star point, string only 20 beads on after the stitch and pass back through the first eight.

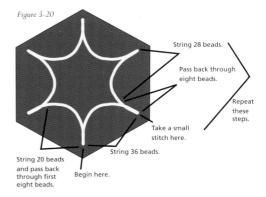

Figure 3-20

String 28 beads.

Pass back through eight beads.

Repeat these steps.

Take a small stitch here.

String 36 beads.

String 20 beads and pass back through first eight beads.

Begin here.

6. To begin the next set of loops, take a small stitch in the fabric, then pass back up through the eight beads and five more beads in the loop to the left. Now working to the right as shown in Figure 3-21, *string 10 beads then pass through the 10 center beads in the next loop to the right, repeat from asterisk around.

7. Pass through the first four beads in the next 10-bead loop to begin the next round.

8. String on five seed beads, as in Figure 3-22, and pass back through two beads in the center of the next 10-bead loop created in step 6. Repeat around the center.

9. String on 3" of seed beads and pass around the 10-bead loops from step 6, as shown in Figure 3-23, to create the twisted effect in the star

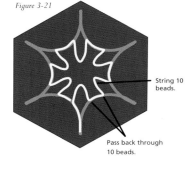

Figure 3-21

String 10 beads.

Pass back through 10 beads.

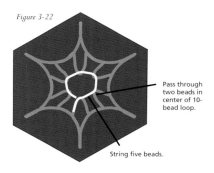

Figure 3-22

Pass through two beads in center of 10-bead loop.

String five beads.

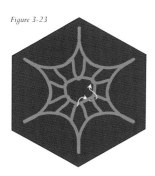

Figure 3-23

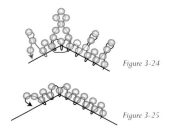

Figure 3-24

Figure 3-25

Assembly

1. Holding both pieces of Ultrasuede together as one, stitch edging pattern from Figure 3-24 along four sides of the suede, making the stitches through both layers of suede, attaching them together.

2. Stitch the edging pattern from Figure 3-25 along the remaining two sides of suede, stitching through just one layer so you have an opening in the bag.

3. Thread needle with at least an 18" length of thread and attach at one corner of the opening of the bag to begin the twisted chain hanger.

4. String a 6½" length of beads and pass through the other corner of the bag.

5. String another 6½" length of beads and pass under the first strand over and over again, until the strands are twisting around each other smoothly.

6. Attach the strand to the opposite corner of the opening.

7. Weave in ends.

Figure 3-26

Flower Sampler

Flowers are fun to make with beads because with all the different colors and shapes of beads, you have the opportunity to create every kind of flower from realistic to fantastic. Here are just a few samples of flower ideas using specialty beads to form many of the shapes. Use these or make up your own creations to keep as a reference for future projects.

Finished Size

Fits a 5½" frame opening

Stitches Used

Straight
Leaf
Picot

Materials

*Various leaf, seed and pressed glass beads (look for beads similar those used; some are vintage and therefore the exact beads may be difficult to find)

*Beading needle and thread to match fabric or beads

*10" square of printed fabric

*Picture frame with 5½" square opening

*8" round embroidery hoop

*Ironing board and iron

*Fabric marker

Instructions

1. Lightly outline just beyond the center 5½" square section of the fabric so you will know to keep your flowers in that area.

2. Place fabric in hoop.

3. Stitch the flowers as shown in Figure 3-27 on the next page, placing them as shown in the photograph sample below or arranging them as you like.

Assembly

1. Remove the fabric from the hoop and press where the hoop wrinkled the fabric.

2. Cut the fabric so it extents about 1" beyond the frame opening.

3. Wrap the fabric around the cardboard that comes with the frame (or cut a piece of cardboard to fit the frame if it didn't come with one), and tape it in place, being careful to keep the stitching centered. Insert in frame.

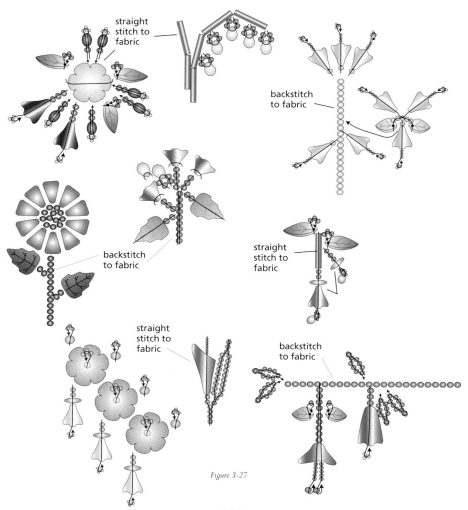

Figure 3-27

Pastel Blue Pulled Thread Sampler

This straightforward design is an example of what you could do with any of the stitches presented throughout this book. Just take all the ones you want to try or think are fun and interesting, work them up in rows, and find a decorative frame to show them off. Here I have chosen a combination of pulled thread stitches with beads incorporated into the designs and straight stitches of beads to accent the designs as well.

Finished Size
To fit a 5" x 7" frame

Stitches Used
Pulled Thread

Materials
- 28 grams cream size 11 seed beads
- Size 8 cream pearl cotton
- 7" x 9" piece pale blue evenweave linen
- 5" x 7" piece purple decorative paper
- Picture frame with 5" x 7" opening
- Ironing board and iron
- Basic sewing supplies

Instructions
See Figure 3-28 on the next page for direction in how to make the stitches, as referenced in parentheses in the step-by-step text below.

1. Begin about 1½" down from the top edge of the fabric and work the half cross stitch over six threads in one direction, stringing two beads for each stitch and pulling the stitches tightly to form the holes in the fabric (1). Work the next row of half cross stitch in the opposite direction.

2. Skip six horizontal threads and pull out the next six horizontal threads. Skip the next six horizontal threads and pull out the next six horizontal threads.

3. Stitch Italian hem stitch variation over the center six horizontal stitches, adding the beads as shown (2).

4. Skip 12 stitches and work faggot stitch (3) over the next 18 horizontal stitches, working over six stitches for each repeat of the pattern.

5. Add the three bead picots to every other top stitch after completing the faggoting.

6. Whipstitch the bottom row, adding one bead with each stitch.

7. Skip nine horizontal threads and work two rows of diagonal chained border, spacing them 16 horizontal threads apart and adding one bead in each stitch as shown (4) on the first row.

8. Add the straight stitch details on the second row, after completing the row in step 7.

9. Skip 10 horizontal threads and pull out the next six horizontal threads.

10. Work one row of hem stitch over six vertical and six horizontal stitches, adding a bead to each stitch as shown (5).

11. Skip eight horizontal stitches and pull out the next six horizontal stitches.

12. Work one row of zigazag hem stitch with no beads (6).

13. Skip four horizontal stitches and work one row of four-sided stitch, adding beads as shown (7).

Assembly

1. Steam press the design from the wrong side.

2. Insert in the frame, centering from top to bottom, with the colored paper behind so it shows through the pulled thread areas of the design.

Figure 3-28

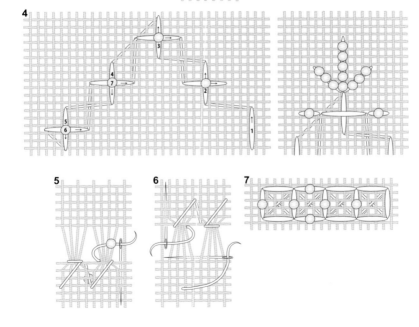

(shown worked over 4 threads)

(shown worked over 4 threads)

Lavender Sampler

Projects that stitch up quickly are always fun to make. You can enjoy your stitching and have it on the wall in a weekend! This little sampler has a little bit of several things, from adding beads to a stitch pattern, to using pressed glass beads for a quick and easy flower accent, to putting a small dangle on the canvas. You can follow the pattern shown, or change a few colors or stitches to make it uniquely yours.

Finished Size ☙

2" x 4½" stitched area

Stitches Used ☙

Backstitch   Florentine
Lazy Daisy   Slanting Gobelin
French Knot   Cross

Materials

◦24 pale blue size 15 seed beads (2)*

◦16 purple size 15 seed beads (8, 10)*

◦5 purple size 11 seed beads (10)*

◦3 purple ¼"-long faceted oval beads (8, 10)*

◦4 pale green ⅛" wedge-shaped beads (8)*

◦1 purple ³⁄₁₆" flower bead (8)*

◦Beading needle and thread
to match fabric or beads

◦3" x 6" rectangle 18-count purple canvas

◦1 skein size 5 variegated sky blue
pearl cotton (3)*

◦1 skein size 8 orchid pearl cotton (1, 7)*

◦1 skein size 12 variegated purple
pearl cotton (4, 9)*

◦1 skein size 12 variegated green-and-purple
pearl cotton (2)*

◦2 yards dark purple ⅛"-wide
woven embroidery ribbon (5)*

◦1 skein medium green silk/wool
embroidery thread (6)*

◦1 skein pale green silk/wool
embroidery thread (10)*

◦1 skein variegated blue-and-purple
silk/wool embroidery thread (10)*

◦1 skein variegated cream-and-green
silk/wool embroidery thread (6, 10)*

◦Size 8 metallic purple cord (1)*

◦Picture frame (mat to fit 2" x 4½" stitched area)

◦Scissors

Instructions

Following Figure 3-29, use beading needle and thread to stitch the rows of pattern stitches on the canvas, adding the beads as shown. *Note: The numbers in parentheses in Materials list refers to number in Figure 3-29 where that item is used.

Assembly

Insert the finished needlework into the frame.

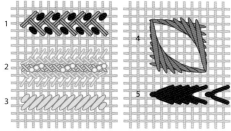

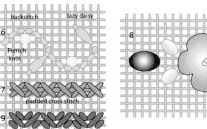

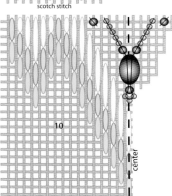

Figure 3-29

Pink-and-Purple Wall Ornament

Simple needlepoint stitches are enhanced with beads, as shown in this design that includes everything from tiny size 15 seed beads to Swarovski crystals and pressed-glass flower beads. The large pressed-glass flowers, which are commonly used in hanging designs, are held in place by attaching their stamens to the canvas, so they can be placed in all directions. Easy stem stitch creates the rope-like bead border.

Materials

- 14 grams cream size 11 seed beads
- 14 grams iridescent clear size 11 seed beads
- 7 grams purple size 11 seed beads
- 7 grams light green size 15 seed beads
- 7 grams medium green size 15 seed beads
- 7 grams iridescent clear ¼" bugle beads
- 7 grams purple sizes 8 triangle beads
- 4 green 4mm Swarovski crystals
- 24 cream size 8 seed beads
- Beading needle and thread to match fabric or beads
- 1 skein green silk/wool blend embroidery thread
- 1 skein variegated cream/green/blue/lavender silk/wool blend embroidery thread
- 1 skein light salmon six-strand embroidery floss
- 1 skein medium salmon six-strand embroidery floss
- 5" x 6" piece natural color 18-count evenweave cloth
- Scrap printed fabric to match thread and bead colors
- Picture frame with 6" x 7" or larger opening
- Sewing needle and thread to match fabric
- Ironing board and iron
- Fabric marker
- Scissors

Finished Size
5¼" x 6¼" stitched area

Stitches Used
Tent
Cross
Satin
Scotch
Straight
Slanted Gobelin
Stem

Cutting Plan
From the printed fabric, cut as follows:
- two 2" x 6" strips
- two 2" x 7" strips

Instructions

1. Using the embroidery threads and following the pattern in Figure 3-30b, stitch the top border stripes and the central design, adding the accent beads as shown in Figure 3-30a.

Figure 3-30a

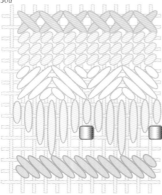

2. Trim the canvas to three threads beyond the needlework on all sides.

3. Line up one of the shorter 2" strips of fabric with the long side edge of canvas, right sides together, and backstitch through both thicknesses along the third hole of canvas from the edge. Repeat for the other long side of the canvas with the remaining shorter 2" strip.

4. Turn the fabric to the right side and press the fold of the seam.

5. Trim top and bottom strips of fabric so they are flush with the top and bottom canvas edges.

6. Line up one of the remaining 2" strips of fabric with the top of the canvas edge and side fabric strips, right sides together, and backstitch as in step 3, continuing the backstitch along the fabric along the sides of the piece.

7. Turn the strip to the right side and steam press the folded seam.

8. Repeat steps 6 and 7 with the last strip on the bottom edge of the canvas.

9. Lightly mark a rectangle on the fabric, ½" from the canvas.

10. Make a stem stitch border along the marked rectangle using seven beads to fill each stitch, alternating with the cream and clear iridescent size 11 seed beads.

11. Make straight stitches fanning out from the corners of the stem stitch border.

12. String one size 8 cream seed bead and three size 11 cream seed beads in the centers of each fan shape. Pass back through the size 8 seed bead, entering the fabric in the same place where you started the stitch. Repeat for each corner.

Assembly

Insert your finished beadwork into the picture frame.

Figure 3-30

- ☐ unstitched canvas
- ▨ 3-strand floss, pink tent stitch
- ▨ 2-strand wool, green, cross stitch
- ▭ ¼"-long bugle bead
- ▯ size 8 triangle bead
- ◙ size 11 seed bead, purple
- ◖ size 11 seed bead, cream
- ◉ size 15 see bead, green
- ◉ size 15 seed bead, pale green

Bargello Glasses Case

This little case shows how well beads can work in needlepoint designs. You can use this piece as a glasses holder on your nightstand, but it doubles just as well holding crochet hooks or double-pointed knitting needles in your knitting or crochet basket. If you leave it unfolded and add a backing, you can make a nice straight knitting needle holder as well.

Finished Size ☞
3¼" x 5¾" case

Stitches Used ☞
Tent

Backstitch	Slanted Gobelin	Scotch
Bargello	Straight	Looped Border

Materials

- 28 grams cream size 11 seed beads
- 7 grams green size 11 seed beads
- 7 grams salmon size 15 seed beads
- 7 grams green size 11 seed beads
- 7 grams bronze size 11 seed beads
- Beading needle and thread to match fabric or beads
- 1 ball light salmon size 12 pearl cotton
- 1 skein variegated greens size 12 pearl cotton
- 1 skein each six-strand embroidery floss, as follows:
  - cream
  - pale pink
  - salmon
  - pale yellow
  - gold
  - light green
- 1 skein variegated cream/yellow/brown/blue size 12 pearl cotton
- 1 skein variegated green-and-salmon silk/wool blend embroidery thread
- 1 skein variegated cream/pale pink/pale green/pale blue silk/wool blend embroidery thread
- 1 card light salmon mohair blend embroidery thread
- 1 skein metallic gold six-strand embroidery floss
- Tapestry needle
- Blunt-ended bead embroidery needle
- 3½" x 12" piece 18-count evenweave canvas
- 3½" x 14" piece lining fabric
- Ironing board and iron
- Scissors
- Straight pins

Instructions

1. Fold the top edge of the canvas over three stitch widths and press in place.

2. Use four strands of variegated green size 12 pearl cotton to stitch the fold in place with vertical straight stitches over three threads as in Figure 3-31.

3. Work loops of six beads (two pink, one green, three pink) in every other stitch along the top edge of the fold. String one pink bead in and out of each green bead as in Figure 3-31.

4. Backstitch one green bead in each stitch along the bottom row of straight stitch.

5. Work the zigzag bargello pattern, using beading thread to add the three-bead stitch after the dark green row.

6. Stitch the center slanting gobelin stripe and then the Scotch stitch along the sides without beads.

7. Stitch the light green tent stitch section and the long bargello pattern on the remaining canvas, following Figure 3-32. Work section A first from top to bottom, followed by section B from bottom to top and then section C from top to bottom.

8. Add the slanting beads on the center gobelin stripe using beading thread.

9. Add beading to the Scotch stitch using one strand of the size 12 pearl cotton that was used to create the Scotch stitch.

Assembly

1. Trim the canvas to two threads beyond the stitching.

2. Turn one short end of the lining over ½" and press.

3. Line up short end from step 2 with top end of the canvas, wrong sides together, so the sides of both pieces are flush and the fold of the lining extends a little above the bead edging on the canvas (so your glasses won't get scratched by the beads when you put them in and take them out of the case). Sew in place with small backstitches on the inside of the lining, about ⅛" from the fold.

4. Pin the lining to the back of the canvas.

5. Backstitch along the bottom fold line to hold the fold in place and baste along the sides.

6. Remove the pins and trim any excess lining flush with the canvas.

7. Use four strands of size 12 pearl cotton to buttonhole stitch along the sides of the case, stitching through both layers to attach them together.

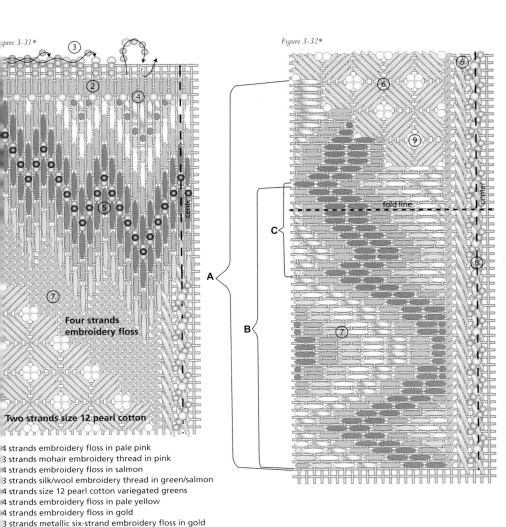

Figure 3-31*

Figure 3-32*

Four strands
embroidery floss

Two strands size 12 pearl cotton

fold line

4 strands embroidery floss in pale pink
3 strands mohair embroidery thread in pink
4 strands embroidery floss in salmon
3 strands silk/wool embroidery thread in green/salmon
4 strands size 12 pearl cotton variegated greens
4 strands embroidery floss in pale yellow
4 strands embroidery floss in gold
3 strands metallic six-strand embroidery floss in gold
4 strands size 12 pearl cotton in variegated cream/yellow/brown
1 strand silk/wool embroidery thread in cream/pink/green/blue

*The circled numbers indicate the step in the instructions on page 216.

Beading Sampler Pincushion

This very Victorian design is a mixture of beadwork stitches that look like a miniature ottoman, complete with ruffled or fringed trim along the bottom. The beaded flowers in the corners of the Aida cloth are easy to create, and the transition of beadwork stitches is a great introduction to learning the most common stitches in beadwork.

Finished Size

2" x 2" x 1¼" pincushion

Stitches Used

Backstitch

Leaf

Classic Edging

Peyote

Right-Angle Weave

Brick

Herringbone

Materials

- 14 grams matte purple size 11 seed beads
- 7 grams dark blue size 11 seed beads
- 7 grams metallic burgundy size 11 seed beads
- 7 grams matte bronze size 11 seed beads
- 7 grams gold size 11 seed beads
- 7 grams green size 11 seed beads
- 7 grams transparent purple size 11 seed beads
- 7 grams metallic blue/black size 11 seed beads
- 7 grams green size 15 seed beads
- 7 grams rose size 15 seed beads
- 7 grams purple size 15 seed beads
- Beading needle and thread to match fabric or beads
- 5" square tan 14-count Aida cloth
- 2" square black velvet
- 9" x 12" piece cream felt
- 2" square of Ultrasuede
- Scissors

Instructions

1. Follow Figure 3-33 to work the beadwork stitches along one side of Aida cloth. Repeat for the other three sides.

2. Cut the center of the Aida cloth and trim the raw edges.

3. Fold under and stitch the opening to the velvet.

4. Work one row of classic bead edging stitch along the fold of Aida cloth.

5. Stitch the bead leaves and flowers in each corner of the Aida cloth, as in Figure 3-34.

Assembly

1. Trim the outer edges of Aida cloth to ½" beyond the last row of beadwork.

2. Fold the corners in and stitch the sides of beading together, weaving in and out of the side beads and adding a bead to complete the pattern on the right-angle weave section of the beadwork.

3. Fold the excess Aida cloth up to the inside of the beadwork.

4. Cut about 10 1¾" felt squares and stack enough of them in the beaded form to create a firm box shape, slightly rounded on top.

5. Tack the felt in place by stitching back and forth across the bottom of the Aida cloth in all directions to hold everything in place.

6. Stitch the Ultrasuede to the bottom of the completed pincushion.

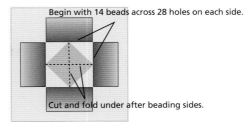

Begin with 14 beads across 28 holes on each side.

Cut and fold under after beading sides.

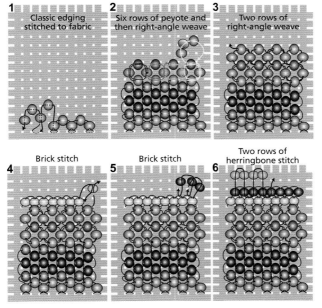

1 Classic edging stitched to fabric

2 Six rows of peyote and then right-angle weave

3 Two rows of right-angle weave

4 Brick stitch

5 Brick stitch

6 Two rows of herringbone stitch

Figure 3-33

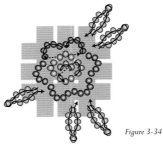

Figure 3-34

Batik Leaves Lingerie Bag

Many batik fabrics have beautiful, subtle printed designs that you can greatly enhance by a little beaded outline to bring out the pattern. This very simple bag is made more elegant with the easy beadwork touches and the luscious, embroidered satin lining. By changing the fabric and lining, you can adapt this basic pattern to any kind of bag, from a shoulder bag to a needlework storage holder. The leaf pattern from the fabric I used is included so you can also work this pattern on a solid fabric or on a print that doesn't have a specific design to follow.

Finished Size ☺
12½" x 10½" bag when closed

Stitches Used ☺
Backstitch
Straight
Brick

Materials
* 14 grams matte purple AB size 11 seed beads
* 14 grams matte brown AB size 11 seed beads
* 14 grams matte purple AB size 8 seed beads
* Beading needle and thread to match fabric or beads
* Embroidery hoop
* 14¼" x 27¾" piece batik fabric with printed design to outline in beads
* 14¼" x 27¾" piece lining fabric
* Pencil
* Sewing machine and thread to match fabric
* Ironing board and iron
* Basic sewing supplies

Instructions
1. Plan ahead to ensure your beadwork will end up on the bag flap. To do this, fold your fabric into thirds, adjusting the last fold so it is shorter like the finished bag shape. Find a design in the flap part of your fabric that you want to outline with beads and place that in the center of the hoop. If you are using the leaf pattern (Figure 3-35 on the next page) on solid fabric, lightly draw the design on the fabric with pencil.

2. Using backstitch and straight stitch, stitch the outline of the pattern, beginning with the outer outlines and then working the inside lines. For the backstitches, string about three to four beads for each stitch, passing through the last bead strung to prepare for the next stitch.

Assembly

1. Use Figure 3-36 to create a bag pattern and cut the beaded fabric and the lining into shape.

2. Pin the pieces right sides together.

3. Begin at the inside edge and machine stitch the pieces together with a ½" seam, leaving an 8" turn-hole at the inside edge.

4. Trim the corners and notch the curve of the flap.

5. Turn right side out and press stitched edges flat.

6. Handstitch the inside edge opening closed.

7. Fold the bag into the finished shape, as in Figure 3-37, and pin the sides together.

8. Stitch the sides together with one row of brick stitch, using the size 8 seed beads. Weave in ends.

Figure 3-37

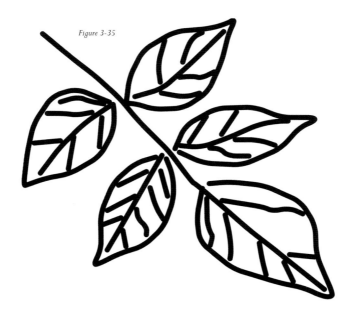

Figure 3-35

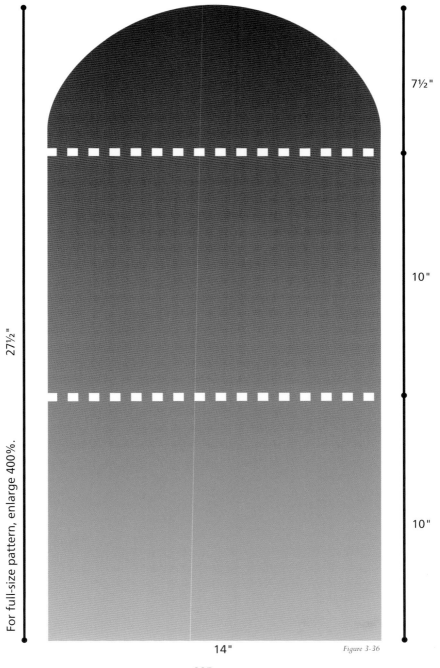

7½ "

10 "

27½ "

10 "

For full-size pattern, enlarge 400%.

14 "

Figure 3-36

Fall Hues Shoulder Bag

Patchwork squares and stripes form this great backdrop for lots of crazy quilt bead embroidery. The rich colors inspire festive beading stitches. And the purchased satin quilted lining makes the finished bag luxurious and sturdy — a wonderful bag to hold you next favorite needlework project.

Finished Size

15" x 12" shoulder bag with 1½" x 26" straps

Stitches Used

Crazy Quilt

Tips for Success

Use ¼" seam allowance on all patchwork and ½" seam allowance on all assembly.

Materials

- 28 grams matte gold size 8 triangle beads
- 14 grams red size 11 seed beads
- 14 grams green size 11 seed beads
- 14 grams gold size 8 seed beads
- Embroidery needle and size 8 pearl cotton to match or contrast fabric
- 18 2" x 72" fabric strips (two each of nine colors)
- 18" x 14" quilted lining fabric
- 2" x 27" brown lining fabric
- Sewing machine and thread to match fabric
- Ironing board and iron
- Basic sewing supplies

Instructions

Narrow Diagonal Strip Section

1. Cut 9" off each of the 2" x 72" fabric strips and then cut the 9" strips in half lengthwise, as in Figure 3-38.

2. Sew the 9" strips together, offsetting them about 1½" as in Figure 3-39.

3. Cut the pointed edges of the finished piece off, as in Figure 3-39, so you have a 2¼" x 26" strip of diagonal fabrics.

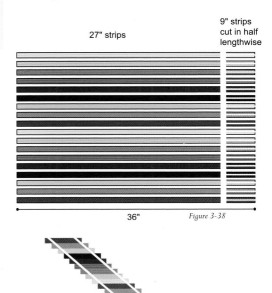

27" strips

9" strips cut in half lengthwise

36"

Figure 3-38

Figure 3-39

Squares and Stripes

1. Arrange the remaining long strips in the order you want them and sew the long sides together with ¼" seam allowance so you have one large striped rectangle of fabric.

2. Sew the long sides of the rectangle together, as in Figure 3-40, so you a have a tube.

3. Fold the tube in half and cut seven 2" strips off the tube, as in Figure 3-41. Set three aside for the shoulder straps.

4. Sew one of the remaining four strips to the long tube, offsetting the colors by one. Repeat for the next three strips so you end up with a tube that looks similar to the finished bag.

5. Decide where you want the top of the bag and unseam that row of stitching, as in Figure 3-42.

6. Sew the narrow diagonal strip section to the bag, again shown in Figure 3-42, on the end with the long strips.

Shoulder straps

1. Cut the three strips in half lengthwise.

2. Sew three of the strips together, offsetting them by one color as you did for the bag. Repeat for the remaining three strips.

3. Unseam the strips, as in Figure 3-43, where you want them to attach to the bag.

4. Pin one strip and brown lining right sides together and sew the long sides together. Repeat for the other strip and lining.

5. Turn right-side out and press.

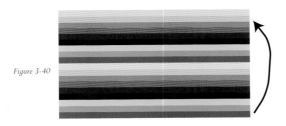

Figure 3-40

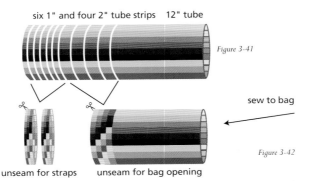

six 1" and four 2" tube strips   12" tube

Figure 3-41

sew to bag

Figure 3-42

unseam for straps   unseam for bag opening

Figure 3-43

Beadwork

1. Work the crazy quilt stitches on the front of the body of the bag as shown in the Figure 3-44 stitch illustrations below, or have fun experimenting with any stitches from the book. Refer to photo on page 226, if needed.

2. Leave the edges unbeaded so you can machine stitch them together.

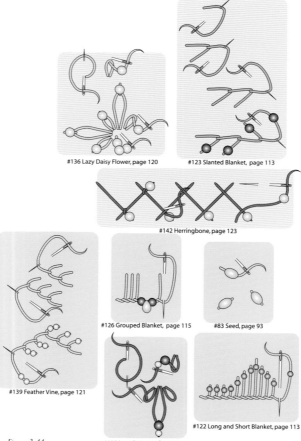

#136 Lazy Daisy Flower, page 120

#123 Slanted Blanket, page 113

#142 Herringbone, page 123

#126 Grouped Blanket, page 115

#83 Seed, page 93

#139 Feather Vine, page 121

#122 Long and Short Blanket, page 113

Figure 3-44

#135 Lazy Daisy Leaf, page 119

Assembly

1. Sew the side seams of the beaded bag together and then sew the straps to the bag, as shown in Figure 3-45.

2. Sew the lining side seams, as in Figure 3-46.

3. Pin the bag inside the lining, right sides together, and sew around the top edge, leaving an 8" turn-hole.

4. Turn right-side out and press seam so the lining is slightly inside the bag.

5. Topstitch around the opening of the bag.

Figure 3-45 (bag)

4"

4½"

about 2½"

**Sew seams and straps
and turn right-side out**

Figure 3-46 (lining)

½"

about 2½"

**Sew seams
leave inside-out**

Vintage Ribbon Bag

Beautiful vintage ribbon deserves special treatment with bead embellishment and detail. This lined purse, with its hand carved inlaid handles, began with the ribbon. By choosing beads, fabric and the handles to complement the ribbon, it's easy to make a beautiful project.

Finished Size
8½" x 7½" purse, not including handles

Stitches Used
Fringe and Edging
Peyote

Materials
* 7 grams silver-lined gold size 11 seed beads
* 7 grams matte lavender size 11 seed beads
* 6 grams gold aurora borealis large Delica beads
* 24 gold ¼" faceted beads
* 16 gold ½" tapered beads
* 40 matte lavender oval three-sided beads
* Beading needle and thread to match fabric or beads
* 2 20" squares printed fabric
* 9" length 2¾"-wide vintage ribbon
* 12" length ¾"-wide ribbon
* ¼" x 2" rectangular shell or bead
* 4" length ⅜"-wide ribbon
* ½-yard fabric
* ½-yard lining fabric
* Purse handles
* Sewing machine and thread to match
* Basic sewing supplies

Cutting Plan
1. From fabric, cut as follows:
   * two front and bag bag pieces, using the pattern on page 235
   * two 9¼" x 4¼" side pieces
   * one 9¼" x 4¼" bottom piece
2. From lining fabric, cut as follows:
   * two front and bag bag pieces, using the pattern on page 235
   * two 9¼" x 4¼" side pieces
   * one 9¼" x 4¼" bottom piece

Instructions
1. Handstitch the ribbon pieces to the front section of the bag as indicated on the pattern.
2. Sew the front, back and sides to the purse bottom, as in Figure 3-47. Repeat for the lining pieces.
3. Sew the side pieces of the purse together, as in Figure 3-47. Repeat for the lining pieces.

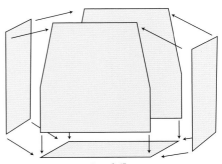

Figure 3-47

4. Stitch the bead patterns onto the ribbon on the front of the purse, as in Figure 3-48.

5. Glue the ⅜"-wide ribbon to the end of the shell. Let dry.

6. Stitch the bead pattern to the ribbon on the shell as in Figure 3-49 and the pattern for the edge of the bag as in Figure 3-50.

Bead Key

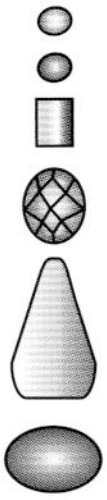

size 11 seed beads
size 11 seed beads
large Delica beads
¼" faceted beads
½" tapered beads
oval three-sided beads

¾" ribbon
2¾" ribbon

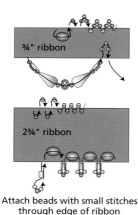

Attach beads with small stitches through edge of ribbon

Figure 3-48

ribbon
loop

Figure 3-50

⅜" ribbon
shell

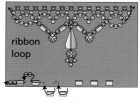

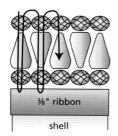

Figure 3-49

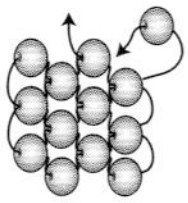

strap

Figure 3-51

Assembly

1. Place the purse inside the lining and pin the top edges together.

2. Seam together, leaving a 6" turn-hole.

3. Turn right-side out by pulling through the 6" hole and press the seam.

4. Stitch the turn-hole closed.

5. Make the beaded peyote stitch straps, as in Figure 3-51, about 2½"-long (or long enough to pass through handle and back of fabric).

6. Sew one end of each beaded strap to the purse, thread through the handle hole and then sew the other end to the purse. Repeat for each handle hole.

For full-size pattern, increase 200%.

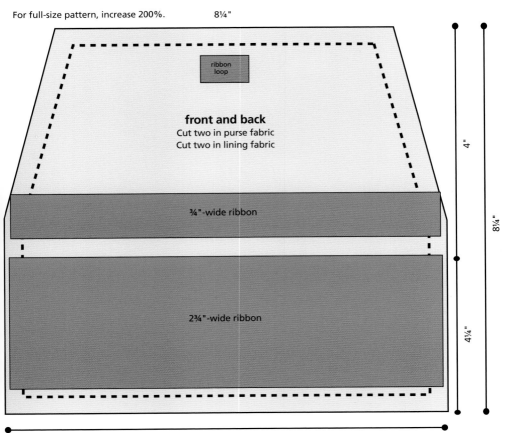

8¼"

ribbon loop

front and back
Cut two in purse fabric
Cut two in lining fabric

¾"-wide ribbon

2¾"-wide ribbon

4"

8¼"

4¼"

9¼"

Brown Gathered Bag

Solid-colored fabrics that have tone-on-tone patterns like the one in this bag are the perfect starting point for color fun in beaded backstitch couching techniques. Think of the fabric as a black-and-white drawing that you get to enrich with the color and texture of beads. By using a thick fabric for this project, you can avoid adding a lining. The handle casing can be made, as shown, with the handles inserted partway through the casing, or at the ends of the casing as the instructions describe.

Finished Size
9" x 14" bag, not including handles

Stitches Used
Backstitch

Seed

Straight

Tips for Success
You can also use the pattern shown for the flower design on your own solid-colored fabric by drawing the main lines of the design on your fabric and stitching the beads as shown.

Materials
* 7 grams each three different green colors size 11 seed beads
* 7 grams each three different red colors size 11 seed beads
* 7 grams bronze-gold size 11 seed beads
* Beading needle and thread to match fabric or beads
* ½-yard thick tone-on-tone fabric
* Embroidery hoop
* 2 9½" x ⅜" dowels with ball ends (stained and/or varnished, if desired)
* 2 purse handles with ½" holes
* Sewing machine and thread to match
* Wood glue
* Basic sewing supplies

Cutting Plan
1. Choose the front fabric piece by carefully finding the part of the fabric that you want to embroider. Before cutting out the pieces, make sure you will be able to fit the front piece in the embroidery hoop. If the cut pattern will be too close to the edge to fit into the hoop, place it in the hoop and embroider it first, then cut out the pattern pieces.

2. From tone-on-tone fabric, cut as follows:
   * one 30" x 4¼" piece (sides/bottom)
   * two pieces using Figure 3-52 pattern on the next page (bag body)

Instructions

1. If using flower design, transfer Figure 3-53 to fabric.

2. Use backstitch to embroider your design. For the flower, begin with the outline of the petals, fill in the petals with straight stitches and then use three-bead seed stitches to fill in the center of the flower. For the leaf, stitch the center stripe of the leaf first and then stitch the rest of the leaf and stem around that.

Figure 3-52

For full-size pattern, increase 400%.

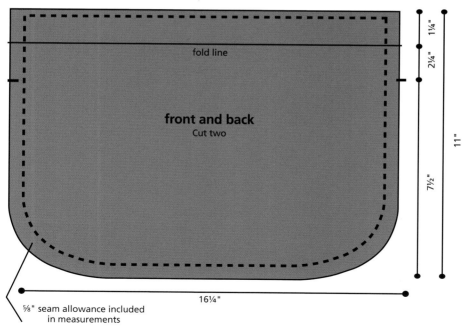

fold line

front and back
Cut two

1¼"

2¼"

11"

7½"

16¼"

⅝" seam allowance included
in measurements

Assembly

1. Fold the short ends of the sides/bottom strip over ½" and then ½" again. Press.

2. Stitch in place and then edge stitch again.

3. Pin the sides/bottom strip to the front of the bag body, matching the center bottom and ending 3½" from the top of the bag on both sides as indicated on the pattern and stitch with a ⅝" seam allowance.

4. Trim the bag seam allowance to ¼", except for the 3½" part at the top.

5. Fold the sides/bottom seam allowance over the ¼" seam allowance and fold the 3½" section along the top of the front under ¼".

6. Seam the 3½" section and zigzag over the folded sides/bottom section, finishing the seam.

7. Repeat steps 3 through 6 for the back of the bag and the other side of the sides/bottom piece.

8. Fold the top edge of the front of the bag over ¼" and then 1" more, press and pin in place.

9. Edge stitch both folded edges in place, creating the casing for the bag.

10. Repeat steps 8 and 9 for the back of the bag.

11. Glue one ball onto each dowel. Let dry.

12. Slide one side of the handles onto each dowel and slide the dowels through the casing, gathering the casing as you slide it on. Slide the other end of each handle onto the dowel.

13. Glue the remaining balls onto the ends of the dowels. Let dry completely.

Figure 3-53

Section 4:
Artists' Gallery

These adorable dolls from Carol Perrenoud's bead embroidery class have bead-embroidered details from head to toe, including twisted fringe hair, classic beaded edging, and crazy quilt and freeform bead embroidery stitches. Notice how Carol enhanced the fabric pattern in the yellow coat by stitching beads on the printed design. Dolls designed and stitched by Carol Perrenoud.

This bead-embroidered doll by Jennifer Gallagher shows a variation of Carol's design with sequins and beads used to accent the fabric pattern in the doll's jacket.

This pin uses couching for the house design, then is embellished on top of the couched beads with bead embroidery, fringe stitches and edging stitches for a three-dimensional effect. "My House" beaded pin, designed and stitched by Carol Perrenoud in size 11 and 14 seed beads with glass cat and bird fetish. This is a project in the "Bead Embroidery Techniques" video by Carol Perrenoud.

This bead-embroidered hat is a great example of taking flower- and leaf-shaped beads (and a ladybug, too!) to create a floral design. Designed and stitched by Jennifer Gallagher for the "Bead Embroidery Techniques" video by Carol Perrenoud.

Tiny antique seed beads and charlottes (seed beads with one side of the bead ground flat so it sparkles in beadwork) were couched into this paisley pattern, then edged with a classic edging. "Paisley Barrette" designed and stitched by Carol Perrenoud in size 16 and 22 antique beads, made in 1990.

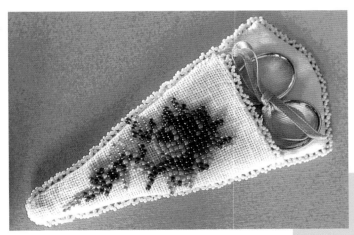

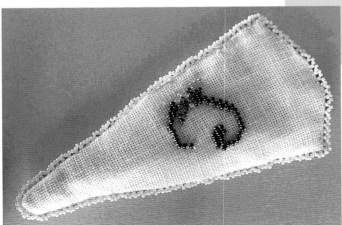

This lovely scissors case was stitched on linen in beaded half cross-stitches, then edged with a classic edging variation. Designed and stitched by Carol Perrenoud. Pattern available from Carol at www.beadcats.com.

This detail of a bead-embroidered vest shows a great way to embellish a fabric pattern with beads. Designed and stitched by Corinne Loomer.

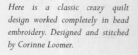

Here is a classic crazy quilt design worked completely in bead embroidery. Designed and stitched by Corinne Loomer.

This cabochon bolo is accented with star-shaped specialty beads. Designed and stitched by Corinne Loomer.

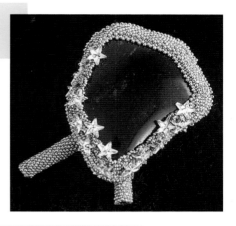

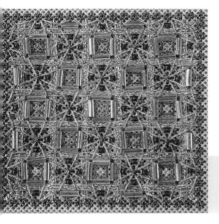

This canvaswork design blends bugle beads and size 11 seed beads with specialty threads. Designed and stitched by Corinne Loomer.

This necklace used couching with size 15 seed beads to create a flower motif. Designed and stitched by Corinne Loomer.

This neckpiece and bracelet are beautiful examples of beaded embroidery used to create flowers. Notice the combination of edgings, fringes and gathering with beads to create the design. "Ultra Flowers" necklace and bracelet designed and stitched by Margo Field. For classes on these projects, visit Margo's Web site at www.poppyfield.com.

The following designs show bead embroidery, mostly backstitch, on leather, designed and stitched by Wendy Ellsworth.

"Monument Valley Purse," designed and stitched by Wendy Ellsworth.

Detail of "Celia's Evening Bag," designed and stitched by Wendy Ellsworth.

"Datura Flower," designed and stitched by Wendy Ellsworth.

"Maroon Bells (Aspen, Colo.) Purse," designed and stitched by Wendy Ellsworth.

"Aztec Shield Purse," designed and stitched by Wendy Ellsworth.

"Celtic Cross Purse," designed and stitched by Wendy Ellsworth.

"Shamanic Dream - Ginny's Purse," designed and stitched by Wendy Ellsworth.

"Mask Purse," designed and stitched by Wendy Ellsworth.

"Dragon Evening Bag," designed and stitched by Wendy Ellsworth.

"Wild Woman's Purse: Shaman's Bag," designed and stitched by Wendy Ellsworth.

Detail of "Wild Woman's Purse: Shaman's Bag." Designed and stitched by Wendy Ellsworth.

Detail of "Wild Woman's Purse: Shaman's Bag." Designed and stitched by Wendy

Supply Sources

I always encourage you to look for local sources for your supplies. Nothing can beat seeing your thread, fabric and beads in person. However, here are some sources of supplies if you need to use mail-order.

Beads ☽☽

Creative Castle
2321 Michael Drive
Newbury Park, CA 91320-3233
(805) 499-1377
www.creativecastle.com

Fire Mountain Gems and Beads
1 Fire Mountain Way
Grants Pass, OR 97526-2373
(800) 423-2319
www.firemountaingems.com

Shipwreck Beads
8560 Commerce Place NE
Lacey, WA 98516
(800) 950-4232
www.shipwreck.com

Threads ☽☽

Coats & Clark
(704) 329-5016
www.coatsandclark.com

The Caron Collection
55 Old South Ave.
Stratford, CT 06615-7315
www.caron-net.com

DMC Corp.
www.dmc-usa.com
Mail-order source for DMC:
Herrschners, Inc.
(800) 441-0838

Other ☽☽

KP Books
700 E. State St.
Iola, WI 54990-0001
(888) 457-2873
www.krause.com

Books ☽☽

When looking for stitches to embellish with beads, I used several books as references. If you want to start searching for more stitches for your beads, here is a list of books I keep in my library.

Anchor Manual of Needlework, Interweave Press, Loveland, Colorado, USA, 1990 New Edition
Originally published in 1958, this is one of those old books that is a treasure to find. It is full of stitches.

Bond, Dorothy. *Crazy Quilt Stitches*. Dorothy Bond, Cottage Grove, Oregon, USA. 1981.
This is a wonderful resource for crazy quilt stitch ideas. I found #147 Rosette in this book.

Christensen, Jo Ippolito. *The Needlepoint Book*. Simon and Schuster, New York, New York. 1999. Revised edition.
This is a great source for all things needlepoint, originally published in 1976.

Kooler, Donna. *Donna Kooler's Encyclopedia of Needlework*. Leisure Arts, Inc. Little Rock, Arkansas, USA. 2000.
This is a great newer book with good photos and illustrations of many stitches.

Snook, Barbara. *Needlework Stitches*. Crown Publishers. Inc., New York, USA. 1972. Fifth printing.
My Aunt Rita gave me this book more than 30 years ago with notes in it on working Hardanger stitches for a bookmark she made for me. It's a great resource of embroidery stitches.

Glossary

Center-drilled: Beads with a hole passing through the center of the bead.

Comanche stitch: See brick stitch, page 142.

Dangle: A single strand or configuration of beads attached at one end to a project. Can be an element in a row of fringe or it can be alone or in a small group.

Drop bead: A bead that is thicker at one end than at the other, which can be side drilled at the small end or can be center drilled.

Edging: Any addition to the edge of a project that is generally narrower than about ½".

Fringe: A group of dangles in a row.

Gourd stitch: See peyote stitch, page 141.

Picot: A small loop, knot or added beads as a decorative element.

Pressed glass beads: Beads that have been pressed into a mold to create a uniform and/or decorative shape, such as flowers, leaves or cubes.

Seed bead: A bead that is smaller than about ¼" and is rounded.

Side-drilled: Beads with the hole drilled through the side of the bead, either the short distance through an oblong bead or through a section of the bead off center.

Tack, tacking stitch: A small stitch used to hold a thread in place.

Threaded: Passing behind another stitch with a new thread, so the new thread alternately shows above and below the stitch.

Turnaround bead: In dangles, the bead or beads at the end of the dangle that are skipped before the needle is passed back through all the rest of the beads.

Twisted fringe, twisted dangle: A dangle or fringe made of dangles that have two strands or a doubled loop in which the strands are twisted around each other. This can be done by wrapping one strand around the other, or by twisting the thread until the strand kinks up on itself and then securing the end of the strand.

Whipped: Passing under another stitch with a new thread, always in the same direction, either top to bottom, or bottom to top.

Stitch Index